Mifflin County
THEN & NOW
A Changing Community Through the Camera's Lens

Written & edited by
FOREST K. FISHER

Contemporary photographs by
NATHANIEL THIERWECHTER

Mifflin County
THEN & NOW
A Changing Community Through the Camera's Lens

Written & edited by
FOREST K. FISHER

Contemporary photographs by
NATHANIEL THIERWECHTER

Published by
The Mifflin County Historical Society
1 West Market Street
Lewistown, PA 17044

Telephone: (717) 242 - 1022
FAX: (717) 242 - 3488
Email: info@mifflincountyhistoricalsociety.org
Web Site: www.mccoyhouse.com

ISBN 9780976343363
Library of Congress Control Number: 2013908409

© 2013 by Forest K. Fisher & Nathaniel Thierwechter
All rights reserved

Table of Contents

Acknowledgment 7

Introductions 8

Around Mifflin County 10

Around Lewistown 70

Lewistown Redevelopment 130

After Thoughts 171

Bibliography 173

Author's Note: William Lewis, an 18th century Pennsylvania Quaker, lawyer, legislator and federal judge, appears in the "Around Lewistown" page headers. He served in the Pennsylvania Assembly when Mifflin became a county, and is Lewistown's namesake.

Acknowledgment

The author and photographer are grateful to the following for help and input into this project. Many provided time lines and shared historical knowledge of the locations or sites around Mifflin County. Others freely shared images, aiding in the cause of preserving the past. Any omissions are completely unintentional.

We wish to thank and acknowledge:

Individuals
Janice and Todge Aumiller
Vesta Aurand
Sara and Mike Buffington
James "Jimmy" Damicantonio
Paul T. Fagley
Ruth Taylor Fagley
Christeena Kearns
William H. "Bill" Logan, Jr.
Genevieve Gregg McCardle
Linda Howell O'Dell
Steve Palm
Jan Snedeker
Rob Sprankle
Mr. & Mrs. Archie Wagner
Robert M. Welham, Sr.
Mr. & Mrs. Robert M. Welham, Jr.
Jon Zimmerman
Bernard Zook, Warden, MCCF

Businesses & Organizations
East Gate Feed & Grain
Friends of the Embassy Theatre
Miller Theatre - Rob Sprankle
The Trolley Car Café - Doug and Marsha Wagner
City Hook & Ladder Fire Co.
United Fire Company
Brooklyn Fire Company

County Historical Societies
Mary Ann Stratton, President
Kish Valley Historical Society

Mifflin County Mennonite Historical Society

A special thanks to the
Mifflin County
Historical Society's
Karen Aurand,
Executive Secretary;
Jean Aurand Laughlin,
Research Librarian
and the Board of Directors
for supporting and making this project possible.

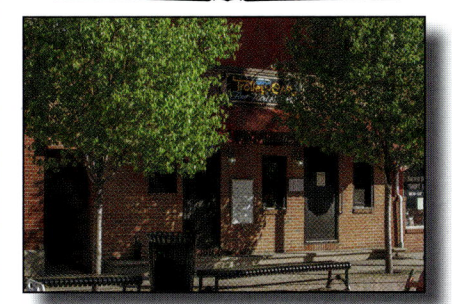

The original Trolley Car, 15 E. Market, shown upper left, was operated by Alfred J. Kellerman in the late 1920s. In 2013, the street facade has changed, but the old car remains part of the establishment.

Historic Photographic Sources

Mifflin County Historical Society Archives - Extensive photo archives cover the history of Mifflin County from the Civil War era to the present, including both negative files and photographic images. In addition, the vertical files of the Society contain newspaper images, engravings, advertisements and other art work. A photo example one might find: Monument Square and trolleys in this pre-First World War view.

The Kepler Studio Collection - The Kepler Studio was owned and operated for sixty years by Luther F. Kepler, Sr. and his brother James A. Kepler, from 1924 until it discontinued operation in the mid-1980s. The business was established on Chestnut Street, and for decades operated as the Kepler Studio & Gift Shop at 127 E. Market Street. The next move was to 28 W. Market, later at 30 N. Dorcas Street beside the YMCA and lastly on the northeast corner of Third and Dorcas. The Kepler Studio Collection consists of negative files from the 1920s (some earlier) through the 1960s, plus black and white photographs, color slides and negatives. The collection is owned by the author. The Kepler Studio is shown here in 1969, at 30 N. Dorcas just prior to its demolition as part of downtown redevelopment.

Most historic photographs are from the Mifflin County Historical Society. Other sources are credited.

Author's Introduction

Fifty years ago my friend Frank Gibboney and I decided we should photograph all the little hamlets and villages in Mifflin Count. Years later we could look back at our photographic chronicle and see how greatly things changed. We would record history.

This goal stemmed from our upbringing, I suppose, and our sense that time brings change, and change can bring an altered landscape. We had an appreciation of our changing community from our elders' "how things were" stories that certainly piqued our sense of history.

Both of us were raised in photographic families; his father, A. Franklin Gibboney III, was a prodigious photographer, well-known in the Reedsville area for decades. Frank's dad grew up near Belleville, and photographed the Kishacoquillas Valley Railroad from the family farm, situated along the Ol' Hook and Eye's right-of-way, until the line ceased operation in 1940.

Luther F. Kepler, Sr., my maternal grandfather, founded a Lewistown studio, later joined by his brother, James A. Kepler, which operated in the downtown for sixty years (1924 to 1984). I draw upon the negatives and prints in the Kepler Studio collection for many local history projects.

Then there was the fact we both had operating darkrooms at our respective homes. Frank and I could each snap photos using black and white film, then develop that film the old fashioned way, with chemical baths - developer, short-stop and fixatives - all accomplished under the warming glow of red filtered darkroom lamps. We were known to burn up film with a vengeance!

After developing the negatives, we could return to those same darkrooms to use photographic enlargers or contact printers to produce positive prints. Again, we used well established chemical processes taught to us by our photographically tech-savvy elders. Even as secondary students, we knew photographic technology could capture our ever-changing community for posterity.

Each time we got together in the years after high school, we commiserated over a recently lost building or new by-pass that altered the landscape. We always declared the worth of shooting those photographs as five years became ten, ten became twenty and twenty pushed fifty.

Sadly, Frank and I never did fulfill our good intentions. This book aims to correct the situation. No darkroom or printers now, times have changed photographically, and that's an understatement!

Collaborating on this project with local photographer Nathaniel Thierwechter has given us the ability to utilize the latest advances in digital photography. Capturing those changes through his discerning lens, allows us to form a unique, comparative view of Mifflin County. The modern views, for the most part, were taken in 2012, a few in 2013.

The Mifflin County Historical Society's photo archives and a number of generous donors who shared their historical photographs, combine to give the reader a glimpse of our past compared to the present.

Although text and captions give brief historical perspective and add to the record, the comparative photos tell the real tale. In this case, a picture is worth a thousand words.

Fifty years in coming, this book is the fulfillment of my personal desire to chronicle our ever-morphing community for future generations. As readers page this book, we trust that each will see and appreciate our changing community through the camera's lens in *Mifflin County - Then & Now*.

Forest K. Fisher

ABOUT THE AUTHOR ....

Born in Lewistown, author Forest K. Fisher was raised in rural Mifflin County. He attended county schools and later Penn State, retiring in 2009 after a 34 year career as a county elementary teacher. He and wife Dot live near Reedsville. His association with the Mifflin County Historical Society began in 1996, when he joined the board of directors. In addition to serving a term as board president and vice-president, he authored a number of society books and publications, and serves as newsletter editor.

Fisher commented on his love of history, explaining, "I was the only child in a multi-generational family for nine years before my brothers were born. I had the full attention of grandparents and a great grandmother born in 1867. Great grandma Kepler's family stories hooked me on history at an early age, no doubt about it. I vividly recall her recollections of the Flood of 1889, and the changes she saw in her lifetime. I'm thankful for that influence."

Anne E. Kepler (1867-1957) with the author in 1954.

Photographer's Introduction

When first asked to take modern photographs representing scenes from old photographs concerning Mifflin County, I was both extremely excited and very humbled. I've always enjoyed looking at old photographs of Lewistown and Mifflin County, especially ones depicting scenes from the '20s through the '50s when Lewistown seemed to have it all; various types of family owned retail stores, department stores, multiple theaters, neighborhood grocery stores, dozens of restaurants and much more. Much of which was contained within five city blocks, from N. Juniata Street to Dorcas St. though businesses continued well onto Valley and Chestnut Streets.

While some scenes, such as the one of Monument Square and The Embassy Theatre were very easy to match up, many required a bit of detective work. What once were Laurel Creek and Potlicker Flats is now the Laurel Creek Reservoir. What was the Mifflin County Airport Hangar is now Hostetler Truck Bodies. But by far the most difficult were the photos of downtown Lewistown from before the 1969-1970 redevelopment.

For me, born in 1985, these photos represented a completely different community. I had never seen the Lewistown Y.M.C.A. in person. I had also never seen McMeen's, Katz, Kauffman's Music and Furniture, the original Friendship Bookstore and dozens of other businesses that were located between Brown and Dorcas Streets. Through the help of street signs present in some of the photographs and members of the community who were around during that time, I believe and hope that every photo from the past has been represented with its modern equivalent accurately.

One of the hardest things about taking the current photographs was the fact that many sections of Lewistown and Mifflin County have changed, some not for the better. With this in mind and while it would have been more enticing to only capture images of the improved parts of town and the well maintained parts of the county, I feel like it would have been a lie. I certainly do no mean to lament on the fact that Lewistown is not the thriving community that it once was as improvements in the past twenty and especially ten years are obvious. And with new sidewalks and many of the telephone and power lines buried under the ground, Monument Square looks better than it has in the 27 years I've been alive. Adding onto that is the continued expansion of infrastructure improvement and a new almost completed park on Dorcas Street commonly referred to as The Five Points. While these improvements are great, I firmly believe that it is the people of this county who must actively seek to make it better. Public funds and organizations are helping pave the way to a better Lewistown but it is private citizens and businesses that will determine the success of our towns and counties future.

At the very least, I hope this book piques the interest of my generation and those younger to see what Lewistown and Mifflin County was like before pre-industrialization, and that Lewistown was an actual thriving community with culture and character. For others, and especially those who remember pre-redevelopment, I hope it sparks a memory; a meal at Dutch's Diner; Sunday Mass at the old Catholic Church; playing basketball with friends at the Downtown Y or a first kiss from a first date in front of the Embassy Theatre.

I personally came to this project from a historical photographer mindset. I want to represent what these scenes looked like on the day I shot them in 2012-2013. Call them a historical record. I tried very hard and with varying success to not only match the angle of the photo from the past but also consider other factors such as the weather conditions, time of day (as displayed by the location of the sun) and time of season. Some liberties were taken such as if a scene was better lit during a different time of day or if it was better and more evenly lit on an overcast day. Hopefully in 50 years another photographer can retake these same shots and there will be even greater town and county improvement. I believe in Lewistown and I believe in Mifflin County.

Nathaniel Thierwechter

ABOUT THE PHOTOGRAPHER ....

Nathaniel Thierwechter is the son of Andrew and Carrie Thierwechter. Born in Lewistown in 1985 he attended local schools and graduated in 2004. He went on to major in Anthropology and graduated from Kutztown University. He attributes his interest of history to his family who have always had an enthusiasm for genealogical history, as well as national and local history. Nathaniel has always had an interest for photography but especially recognizes his cousin Glenn for laying the foundation for his passion for it. Nathaniel has had numerous photographs published in the local quarterly magazine "Common Ground" and is heavily involved with the Mifflin Juniata Arts Council. He currently is a staff photographer for Centre Publications located in Centre County. Nathaniel was elected Board Member of the Mifflin County Historical Society in April of 2013.

"My then photo was taken in 1988," Nathaniel noted, "at the 125th Anniversary of Gettysburg. I was two years old and was, as kids do, going through my mother's purse and found the camera. I knew sliding the one button opened the shutter but I probably didn't know I actually took a photograph. Neither did my parents until they had the roll developed. This was not only my first self portrait but also my first photograph."

Nathaniel Thierwechter with father, Andrew, in the background. - 1988

AROUND MIFFLIN COUNTY

Lewistown Narrows, US 322 - c. 1936

Postcards and souvenirs featured the Lewistown Narrows over the years. The Victorian tea cup and saucer depicts the Juniata River. It was sold by Ball's Book Store, Lewistown.

The **Lewistown Narrows** has been the southern gateway to Mifflin County since the earliest days. What started as perhaps an animal path, later developed into an American Indian trail meandering along the course of the Juniata River. Trappers, traders and pioneer settlers traveled into this section of the Pennsylvania frontier following the primitive trail in the 1750s. Eventually the trails were enlarged to allow for Conestoga wagon traffic. A turnpike was later established between Harrisburg and Pittsburgh in the early 19th century. The first state road into Lewistown followed this route when it was completed on October 31, 1913. In June 1934, a Tyrone, PA contractor began concreting six miles of highway through the Narrows at a cost of $411,417. US 322, the engineering marvel seen today, follows the original American Indian path.

11

TRAVEL HISTORY

Five stages of travel can be recalled here. Concrete covers the old turnpike. Opposite are the ruins of the old canal. The Juniata was once filled with river craft. Across the river is the Pennsylvania Railroad.

The Pennsylvania Historical and Museum Commission originally placed a marker near the former Treaster's Garage, on March 28, 1947 recognizing travel history, from turnpike to canal and railroad.

Photographer's Comment: I'm standing on the concrete barrier to gain the proper height to replicate this shot. Slightly heavier traffic as well.

Mifflin County – THEN & NOW

Old Stone Arch Bridge - c. 1880

What is known locally as The Old Arch Bridge was built in 1813, part of the turnpike connecting Harrisburg and Pittsburgh. The stone span, noted for the absence of a keystone at the apex of the arch, straddles Jack's Creek just east of Lewistown, parallel to routes US 22 and old 322. The stream is quite tranquil in these images, but can rage during flood stage, inundating the venerable span. After the turnpike was abandoned, the structure fell into disrepair; crumbled casements and adjacent buttresses re-

Around Mifflin County

OLD ARCH BRIDGE
The restored stone bridge opposite was built in 1813. It was part of the turnpike from Harrisburg to Pittsburgh. The arch is without a keystone.

duced to piles of rubble, only the graceful arch itself remained. Restorations in the 1930s, 40s, 70s and early 2000s restored the bridge deck, stone sides and stream bank retaining walls. A picnic area with limited parking is available along Jack's Creek Road. On March 28, 1947, the Pennsylvania Historical and Museum Commission placed an official marker along nearby US 22 remembering the history of the Old Arch Bridge.

14 Mifflin County – THEN & NOW

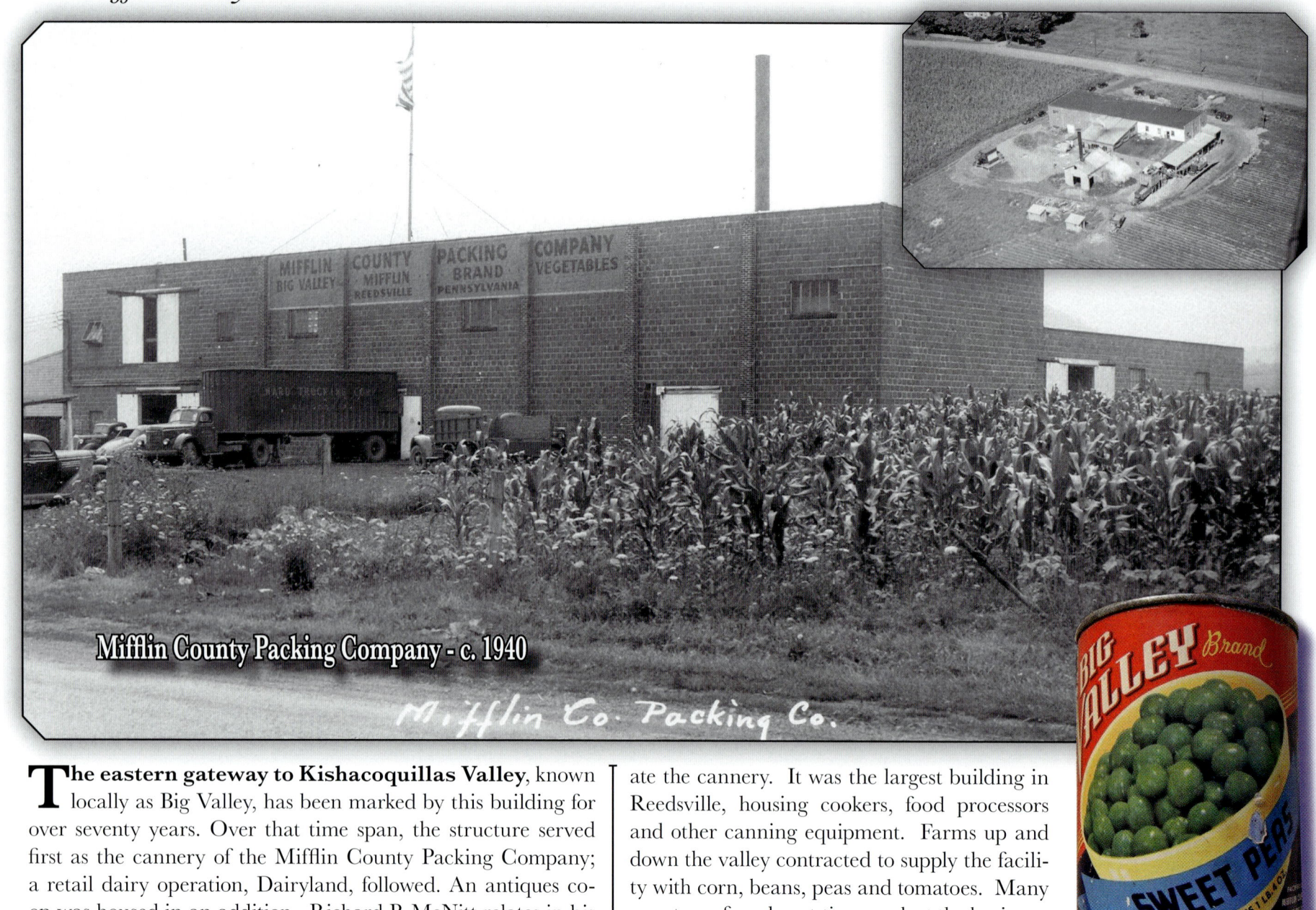

Mifflin County Packing Company - c. 1940

The eastern gateway to Kishacoquillas Valley, known locally as Big Valley, has been marked by this building for over seventy years. Over that time span, the structure served first as the cannery of the Mifflin County Packing Company; a retail dairy operation, Dairyland, followed. An antiques co-op was housed in an addition. Richard P. McNitt relates in his book **Growing Up in Reedsville** that A. Reed Hayes, Roland Thompson and others formed a company to build and oper-ate the cannery. It was the largest building in Reedsville, housing cookers, food processors and other canning equipment. Farms up and down the valley contracted to supply the facility with corn, beans, peas and tomatoes. Many area teens found part-time work at the business, too. The "Big Valley" brand tin can, at right, is from the collection of the Kishacoquillas Valley

Around Mifflin County 15

Historical Society. A devastating fire in 2011 left the original building unsafe, displacing the County Observer office and other tenants. The antiques shops remained open until the end of 2012 with demolition scheduled for 2013, according to reports in the Sentinel (Lewistown, PA). Future plans for the property were not announced as of this printing.   [Sweet pea can & aerial view courtesy Kishacoquillas Valley Historical Society]

16 *Mifflin County – THEN & NOW*

Gibboney Woolen Mill - c. 1940

A Gibboney blanket label from the 20th century.

At the time of its closure, the Gibboney Woolen Mills of Reedsville and Belleville operated continuously for almost 150 years. From its creation in 1801 until it ceased production in 1949, the woolen mill was run by a Gibboney family member, spanning over five generations. The first mill, near Belleville, provided a wool service for local farmers. During the Civil War, the mill manufactured blankets for the Union Army. The operation moved to this location along Coffee Run in 1864. At that time, water powered some new equipment, the first machinery to weave blankets in the Kishacoquillas Valley. This location was called Cedar Hill. As the wool business expanded, another facility was added in Reedsville by World War I. During the 1930s, the Gibboney Woolen Mills operated three shifts with upwards of 85 employees and provided many young local workers with their first real job experience. The woolen mill buildings later housed a number of antiques and craft shops, operating in 2012 as the Old Woolen Mill Shoppes.

18 *Mifflin County – THEN & NOW*

Belleville Hill - c. 1940

Belleville Hill

According to local sources, Belleville was first known as Greenwood, named for blacksmith Joseph Greenwood. The "Postal History of Mifflin County" compiled by George R. Frysinger in 1928, notes that a post office in the village was established in 1800 administered by its first post master, John Reed. Belleville is the

Insets from 1877 *Atlas of Perry, Juniata & Mifflin Counties, Penna.*

principal village in Union Township, established in 1790, the first township established after Mifflin County's founding one year earlier. The name honors the first thirteen states. Treacherous in winter weather, Belleville Hill is on East Main Street, following US 655.

20 Mifflin County – THEN & NOW

Farmers National Bank, Belleville - c. 1920

FARMERS NAT. BANK, BELLEVILLE, PA.

In 1935, the United States Comptroller of the Currency announced in his annual report that the Belleville National Bank and the Farmers National Bank of Belleville (shown above) were consolidated under a corporate charter with the new title of "The Kishacoquillas Valley National Bank." When that banking institution moved out of this building, the Mifflin County Mennonite Historical Society opened its museum in the old Farmers National Bank building. The MCMHS notes on its web site: *Mifflin County Mennonite Historical*

Around Mifflin County

Society is the outgrowth of five years of planning and negotiating by a handful of dedicated Mennonites and Amish, descendants of early settlers to Mifflin County. The Heritage Center doors were opened to the public, October 1988. The former bank building is home to a collection of artifacts from Mennonite and Amish families; a growing collection of genealogy books, cemetery directories, obituaries and much more.

22 Mifflin County – THEN & NOW

West Main Street, Allensville, Pa.

Allensville, future US 655 - c. 1915

Menno Township Business Notices.

Contner D. M., Resident. P. O. Menno.
Peachey Jonathan, Farmer. " "
Peachey J. A., " " "
Weller George, Proprietor Tannery. P. O. Menno.
Wilson J. T., Farmer. P. O. Belleville.

Allensville is a village located in Menno Township at the west end of the Kishacoquillas Valley. The township is named for Menno Simons (1496 - 1561), an Anabaptist religious leader whose

Insets from 1877 *Atlas of Perry, Juniata & Mifflin Counties, Penna.*

followers became known as Mennonites. The village, originally called Horrelton or Horreltown, was laid out in lots in 1806. When

Around Mifflin County

the post office was established it was named after an early settler, Chris Allen, who purchased land when the settlement was established.

Photographer's Comments: While this shot looks simple enough, this was one of the hardest ones as I could not, with total confidence, pinpoint the original photo's location.

24 *Mifflin County – THEN & NOW*

Mann's Narrows – c. 1860

This hand-painted, milk glass plate is decorated with the image of Mann's Narrows, shown here. The unknown artist likely painted this primitive scene in oil in the early 1900s, now somewhat degraded, when such decorative plates were fashionable. A magnifying glass reveals figures along Kishacoquillas Creek, duplicated with the finest of brush strokes. Found among the Aurand-Moore family effects of the late Eleanor M. Aurand, MD, Big Ridge, Lewistown.

Known by various names over the past two hundred-fifty years, this only gap in Jack's Mountain between Mount Union and Union County has been known as Logan's Gap, Mann's Narrows and Reedsville Narrows. Logan, the Mingo chief, resided north of Reedsville when the first pioneers settled the Kishacoquillas Valley before the American Revolution. Later, the Mann Axe Company's multiple structures occupied the gap, harnessing the waters of Kishacoquillas Creek to power the factory. The Milroy Branch of the Pennsylvania Railroad utilized the natural cut through the mountain for its right-of-way, seen at right in the ca. 1860 photograph. The crushed stone roadway in that image reputedly

Around Mifflin County 25

saw rebel spies reconnoitering Mifflin County in June 1863.

Photographer's Comment: This photo was also slightly difficult as I wanted to show the old dirt road that became 322 which is now Mann's Narrows, Kishacoquillas Creek, and the 322 bypass. This is the only spot that allows a clearing in the trees to show all three.

26   *Mifflin County – THEN & NOW*

Honey Creek Inn – c. 1950

Dining room, c. 1960

Author's image - Kepler Studio Collection

This **popular local eatery** had its origins as a gas station lunch counter. Stewart "Lanky" McNitt operated his Esso station along old US 322 in Reedsville. Adjacent to the garage and filling station was a modest restaurant or lunch counter operated by McNitt's wife, Janet. That structure was moved and eventually replaced

Around Mifflin County

with the concrete block restaurant. Honey Creek Inn was operated by others later in the property's existence, including: Stella Johnson, Mr. and Mrs. Donald Kline and Betty Aurand Lawhead. After Honey Creek Inn relocated to Garden View, the building eventually became an Original Italian Pizza restaurant. What first opened as a wayside stop for weary travelers to "fill-er-up" and get a bite to eat, is in 2012 Michelle's Restaurant & Pizzeria serving travelers and regulars alike on the banks of Honey Creek.

28   *Mifflin County – THEN & NOW*

On the western end of Reedsville was the junction of State Route 76 and old US 322. Located near this crossroads was the Reedsville Mill, shown here in 1953, just prior to the realignment of the two roads. The inset below shows Toll Gate Hill, and its namesake, the two-story, slender former toll house of the Belleville Turnpike, or sometimes referred to as the Kishacoquillas Pike. Sign posts indicate State College and Bellefonte, bear to the right beyond the mill, while travelers to Belleville and Huntingdon proceeded left up the hill. There had been a mill on this location since 1775 when the first mill was established by William Brown. Brown's Mill was Reedsville's original name. At the time this photo was made, the water wheel still stood to the left of the mill's main building, obscured by the trees in this view. Noted Pennsylvania historian Dr. Sylvester K. Stevens commented on a destructive mill fire there on October 19, 1959. He noted that this was the longest operating location for milling in this part of Pennsylvania. "Its record in this respect," Stevens reflected, "makes it one of the outstanding mills in the State."

Reedsville Mill - 1953

Author's image - Kepler Studio Collection

After the fire gutted the mill, it was rebuilt as a concrete block structure, operating into the 21st century. Merged with the Belleville Mill in 1997, the Reedsville Mill closed October 1, 2004. In 2012, East Gate Feed and Grain is the mill's business descendant. Considering the importance of milling to a developing community, the former Reedsville Mill site is one of Mifflin County's most historically significant locations.

30 Mifflin County – THEN & NOW

Main Street, Reedsville - c. 1937

Author's image - Kepler Studio Collection

A Lewistown Transportation bus stops for riders in front of the Reedsville National Bank around 1937. The cameraman is standing in the middle of old US 322 looking west, on what was the main route between State College and Harrisburg. Reedsville had not yet acquired a traffic light. Thompson's Hardware is on the right, operated by William Thompson, a fixture in Reedsville for decades, is now but a memory since closing its doors over

Around Mifflin County

a generation ago. The bank became a branch of the Russell National Bank for many years before closing as county banks consolidated. The structure saw service as a youth center, and is a florist today. Thompson's old hardware building was briefly used for church services, later occupied by Reedsville Seafood, and the Main Street Market, 2012.

Inset from 1877 *Atlas of Perry, Juniata & Mifflin Counties, Penna*.

Walnut Street, Reedsville - c. 1938

Author's image - Kepler Studio Collection

Walnut Street, Reedsville before it was paved. This shot was taken about 1938 for a series of town postcards sold at Sankey's Drug Store on Main Street, where Brindle's Paint Store is today. This view shows the Clifford Rice house at the left. The stately home, built by the G. C. Rice family in the early 1900s, boasted an elaborate, wrap-around porch, so typical of homes of that era. Richard P. McNitt writes about Rice's porch in *Growing Up in Reedsville,* "Ideal for the children to play on in inclement weather. One could ride tricycles, wagons and even roller skate on the wooden floor." McNitt mentions that many older Reedsville homes removed or considerably reduced those elaborate porches in size during modernization. The Rice home has no porch today. The large home at the top of Walnut Street in the old view, obscured by trees in the "now" shot, belonged to C. V. Roland, son-in-law of its builder, Alexander Reed. Rowland was publisher of the Sentinel (Lewistown, PA), a principle partner in WMRF radio and Warner Lewis Buick. The building remains one of Reedsville's few brick homes on one of the largest lots in the village, and once boasted an apple and pear orchard.

34 *Mifflin County – THEN & NOW*

Main Street, Milroy - c. 1908

This dirt street was the well traveled thoroughfare through the town, eventually winding its way over the Seven Mountains to Potter's Mills. That village is now in Centre County, but was once part

Inset from 1877 *Atlas of Perry, Juniata & Mifflin Counties, Penna.*

of Mifflin prior to the establishment of final boundaries between the two counties. The Duncan House, located further north on

Around Mifflin County   35

this street, was a stop for stage coaches and travelers. Also note the man-powered wheel borrow mid-street in the vintage view. It is loaded with what appears to be a burgeoning feed sack. The Milroy feed and grain mill was located around the bend off Main Street near the PRR Milroy Branch Station. The architectural feature under the eaves of the two-story structure on the left is a clue to the angle of this pair of photographs.

Mifflin County – THEN & NOW

Milroy - c. 1910

A **horse pauses for a drink** at the original fountain in the center of Milroy, Armagh Township. According to identification on the early photograph, the driver in the vintage automobile is Samuel "Biscuit" Brown, a traveling cracker salesman.

A new fountain replaced an earlier modern version in 2013, including a plaque inscribed: *W. L. BURKE MEMORIAL FOUNTAIN - Dedicated to W. L. "Sonny" Burke for his many years of service to Armagh Township - 2001* (Burke was township supervisor and road master for

Around Mifflin County 37

many years.) American Legion Post 287 generously supported the fountain project, noted the *County Observer* (Reedsville, PA), reporting that the fountain was a project of the Armagh Township Centennial Committee, erected by Glen Boyer and Todd Condo, "for the citizens of the town to enjoy."

Photographer's Comments: Trees once again hide another structure, the house on the hill.

Fountain Square, Milroy - c. 1915

Riders are shown on board the Milroy & Reedsville Transportation Company's bus at the bank building in "downtown" Milroy around 1915. Another view of the fountain, a feature of this Armagh township village that provided a watering hole for passing

Around Mifflin County   39

horses. The Milroy Banking Company office was robbed twice in the 1930s. During the second heist, December 1938, a trio of masked bandits trussed up the cashier, a bank director and a 16 year old customer who just stopped by for change before absconding with $6,500.

The modern view, taken in 2012, shows the second rendition of the fountain erected over a decade earlier and replaced in 2013.

40 Mifflin County – THEN & NOW

Milroy Fire House & Officers - 1940

Fire company officials, 1940

Author's image - Kepler Studio Collection

The Milroy Hose Co. No. 1 was organized on January 16, 1929, according to the company's biography in the 1940 program for the State Firemen's Association Convention held in Lewistown. The company built this two story block building on Milroy's Main Street in March 1929, adding an "L" to the building in 1939 to house the meeting room and a kitchen. About this same time, a "Diamond T" truck with cab was purchased as the company's fire truck.

Photographer's Comments: According to local Milroy historian, Jimmy Damicantonio, the Milroy Branch of the Mifflin County Library's left side, where the entrance is located, is the right part of the old Milroy Hose company truck door. Apparently the rest was lost in a fire.

This location is along old US 322, now the access road to the Municipal Authority's filtration plant at the Seven Mountains reservoir. Don and Louise Wagner's Laurel Run Inn offered travelers a chance to gas up the automobile and grab a bite to eat. Nearby Laurel Run State Park was a popular picnic area until US Route 322 was reconfigured in the early 1970s.

Photographer's Comment: While approaching the former gas station and now house, two ladies on an evening walk passed by and

I asked if either of them lived there. They laughed and with a smile said "No, the Mayor of Pot Licker lives there!" I went to the back door and was greeted by Archie Wagner and his wife, the first family of Pot Licker. Archie told me that his grandparents owned the gas station and restaurant and that it was a big stop for people going to the Laurel Run picnic area that was located nearby. He was able to tell me that this would have been the late 30s or early 40s, before they moved the road closer to the house, which caused the gas pumps to be removed.

44 Mifflin County – THEN & NOW

Mifflin County Airport - 1947

This hangar is shown at the original Mifflin County Airport, organized by ten businessmen interested in aviation. It was constructed in 1947, the next year after the airport was established one-half mile south of Milroy on a farm adjacent to old US 322. Known as the Mifflin County Airport, the county never owned the facility. The first hangar was in an old wagon shed, fitted with an oversized door to accommodate the long airplane wings. A red brick house nearby, that now is home of the Milroy O.I.P., was the residence of the first airport manager, Harvey Hostetler and his family. The airport was at an elevation of 830 feet above sea level, with two

Air Show - MC Airport, July 18, 1948 - "City of Washington" circumnavigated world with pilot George Truman.

Around Mifflin County

runways less than 4,000 feet in length. When the present airport began operation in 1966 near Reedsville, the old buildings were sold.

Photographer's Comments: Believing this was an old hangar at the current airport and worrying about trying to get on the runway, the Federal Aviation Administration and Department of Homeland Security, I was pleasantly informed that, in fact, this structure is located near Milroy and is where Hostetler Truck Body now resides.

46 *Mifflin County – THEN & NOW*

Logan Boulevard - c. 1947

Here's good news - Gulf's "Express Stop" Service Station at Logan Blvd. & Freedom Ave. will open Thursday, June 12th. We have an expertly trained crew ready to give your car the best "Protective Maintenance" services possible. Come in then - won't you . . . and make this your "Service" headquarters.

Gulf Oil Corporation

S. Earl Taylor
Burnham
Pa.

Courtesy Ruth Taylor Fagley

The location was know as "McKim's" or "McKim's Station." There was also a trolley stop there by the same name. Long-time Burnham resident Ruth Taylor Fagley recalled "McKim" as the owner of the gas station at the extreme right, where Mattress World is located in 2012. This image graced an advertising postcard announcing the "new" Gulf Service Center to be built on the opposite corner on W. Freedom Avenue and Logan Boulevard. A second postcard, insets above, was sent when the service station opened for business. The postcards were received by J. Earl Taylor, father of Ruth Fagley, who kindly shared the images. Looking northeast, Standard Steel and Lo-

Around Mifflin County

gan Iron works are in view with Jack's Mountain in the background. The bridge crosses Buck Run, a tributary of Kishacoquillas Creek. At the conclusion of a lengthy replacement process, a new bridge was opened to traffic in 2012.

Photographer's Comments: While this location has changed in certain ways, the mountains haven't and they were what I used to match these two shots together.

St. Patrick's Day Flood - 1936

Rising waters of the **1936** St. Patrick's Day Flood inundate Freedom Avenue with Standard Steel Works and Burnham Borough beyond. Author and historian Paul T. Fagley described elements in the 1936 image. "This is the intersection at Freedom and Logan Blvd. toward the 'hump' bridge," he noted. "On the left is Logan Iron property. The fence is the former Smith Gulf location. The first two buildings were old duplex company houses, owned by Logan Iron." Fagley added that Standard Steel never had any company housing, continuing, "They were torn

Around Mifflin County 49

down when the Uni-Mart was built... to the extreme left (in the old view) the light shaded 2 story building was the passenger station. Also of note, to the right, the second building is a duplex company house, which still exists, next to Creekside Hearth and Patio. The next building was the Logan Iron Boarding House, now the former Cedar House." This neighborhood of Burnham, Fagley reminded, was once known as "Gaptown." When one crossed the hump bridge, the neighborhood was "Yankeetown." Cost of gasoline in 1936? 10 cents a gallon.

Burnham YMCA & Pool Building - 1912

Y.M.C.A., Burnham, Pa.

The Y.M.C.A. at Burnham was founded and incorporated in 1906. The original building, at right, was built at a cost of $22,870 by G. W. Tate of Yeagertown. The building was dedicated on February 12, 1908. Four years later, the gymnasium was enlarged and the swimming pool building added. Furman and Oles Plumbing & Heating, Lewistown (inset) contracted for the swimming pool mechanicals, one of

Around Mifflin County 51

the subcontracts included in the $15,000 expended for additions and improvements. The Burnham School District began using the gym facilities in 1931. Throughout its early history, the Burnham Y greatly appreciated the generous financial and leadership support from Standard Steel Works. Now known as the Juniata Valley YMCA, the organization serves the community on First Avenue.

52 Mifflin County – THEN & NOW

Standard Bakery - c. 1910

The bakery stood on the corner of Beech Street and Sixth Avenue in Burnham. The entrance door opened from the corner of the building. The bakery delivery truck is shown at right in this unidentified photograph. Home delivery of bread, milk and eggs was common at this time. In 1922, Guy S. Beaver together with his two brothers, Ellis and Park, purchased the holdings of the Standard

Bakery, then owned and operated by H. A. Spanogle, and a short time later bought out the Mifflin Bread Company. The officers of the company were: Guy S. Beaver, president; Ellis C., Vice-president; and Park O., secretary and treasurer. The company owned and operated twelve trucks to serve central Pennsylvania. Much later the Econopane window company occupied the location.

54 Mifflin County – THEN & NOW

Kishacoquillas Park - c. 1930s

KISHACOQUILLAS PARK
LEWISTOWN, PA.

Author's image - Kepler Studio Collection

The swimming pool at this central Pennsylvania amusement park near Burnham was a popular attraction for generations. Paul T. Fagley noted in his 2012 book, *Memories of Kishacoquillas Park*, that the sign, "Dance Tonight" on the roof of the bath house was illuminated after dark to help draw in both "hoofers" and amateur dancers alike. The original pool offered a kiddie section located at

Around Mifflin County

the far end in this view. Later, that section would be separated when the pool was rebuilt. The 1972 Tropical Storm Agnes flood forced the pools closure for two years. Derry Township acquired the park in 1974, operating the swimming facility for a number of years until ever increasing operating and repair costs helped bring about its final days as a public pool.

Mifflin County – THEN & NOW

Lewistown Hospital expansion - 1951

Commemorative plate issued forty years ago marking the June 30, 1973 dedication of the hospital's $8 million dollar major expansion and consolidation with the former F. W. Black Community Hospital. The "new" cylindrical portion is still visible in 2012. The postcard features the 1951 expansion and entrance.

Author's image
Kepler Studio Collection

On **May 12, 1951** an open house was held in the new addition to Lewistown Hospital. The occasion was held on National Hospital Day when visitors were given tours of the building, considered at the time as the most up-to-date facility in the county. The day was extended to a full week in 1953, known from then on as National Hospital Week. Contracts were signed in March 1949, noted the *Souvenir Booklet on the History of Lewistown*, totaling over two million dollars for additions and renovations. The hospital was organized February 20, 1905, and expanded periodically over the ensuing century. In a 1947 survey of Mifflin County's resources, Lewistown Hospital had 99 beds, while F. W. Black Community Hospital had 44 beds. The evaluation noted that both were well equipped and staffed. In 2012, the Sentinel (Lewistown, PA) editorialized, "… the hospital is merging with Geisinger Health Systems… We all will benefit from a merger that provides quality, affordable health care for this corner of Pennsylvania."

58   Mifflin County – THEN & NOW

The latest in radiological equipment; food service department, below, both c. 1950

Author's images
Kepler Studio Collection

F. W. Black Community Hospital - c. 1960

Frederick Wallace Black, born in Lenox, Iowa in 1882, served as a battlefield surgeon in Europe during the First World War, advancing the concept of an Army mobile hospital located near the front line fighting, later better known as a MASH unit. Settling in Lewistown after the war, he opened a private hospital at 112 South Main Street for four years prior to breaking ground for this building in 1928. That first building held apartments in recent years. By June 1930, the new F. W. Black Community Hospital on Buena Vista Circle extended an open house to the general public. The insets show the food service department kitchen and the latest in radiological equipment c. 1950. The hospital incorporated as a non-profit institution in 1940, finally consolidating with Lewistown Hospital in 1972. The area Amish community utilized the services at Black's Hospital until the facility closed. The county owned former hospital housed the Mifflin-Juniata Area Agency on Aging offices, but that organization is now located at 249 West 3rd Street, Lewistown. Less the ivy, the building in 2012 has maintained its general appearance.

60   *Mifflin County – THEN & NOW*

Mifflin County Home - c. 1928

Author's image - Kepler Studio Collection

K**nown at one time as** the County Home, the commissioners let a contract in 1928 to A. W. Fink & Co. of Altoona for an addition and remodeling of the "almshouse" at a cost of $69,296. After the facility ceased serving the county's aged residents in the 1970s, the building lay vacant before it was renovated in 1979 to accommodate offices for the Juniata Valley Tri-County Mental Health Mental

Around Mifflin County

Retardation Program (MH/MR) that included Huntingdon, Mifflin and Juniata Counties. The program had been located in the school of nursing building at Lewistown Hospital. The Mental Health Center stayed there for a period of time, while the renovations here were under way. The administrative office moved temporarily to the old library building – currently United Way – on Third Street.

62 *Mifflin County – THEN & NOW*

Main St. Looking North, Yeagertown, Pa.

Yeagertown – c. 1910

Yeagertown marked its 150th anniversary in 1992 with souvenirs like the Yeager Mill feed sack and Mann Axe Factory hatchet lapel pin.

Yeagertown, located along Kishacoquillas Creek, is shown about 1910, then the main line on the Lewistown & Reedsville Electric Railway Company, also the right-of-way for the former Lewistown and Kishacoquillas turnpike traversing Mann's Narrows in Jack's Mountain in the background. This route would eventually become US 322. The town's populace found employment at several in-

Around Mifflin County

dustries, including Standard Steel Works, Mann Axe Factory and the Logan Iron Works. The Yeager Mill along the creek was a prosperous operation owned by local businessman J. M. Yeager.

Photographer's Comments: Once again, the mountains and Mann's Narrows were the key to matching up this Yeagertown shot.

64   *Mifflin County – THEN & NOW*

Mattawana Cemetery - c. 1917

MATTAWANA CEMETARY, MCVEYTOWN, PA.

Inset from 1877 *Atlas of Perry, Juniata & Mifflin Counties, Penna.*

Mattawana Cemetery is located at the north end of McVeytown on US Route 22, on the left upon entering McVeytown Borough from Lewistown. The oldest grave dates from 1858 in this bucolic setting on a hill overlooking the Juniata Valley. It is a large cemetery, divided into four sections, according to *Cemeteries of Mifflin County*, and falls under the category of Oliver Township.

Unfortunately, it has been almost 40 years since the county cemetery reference book has been updated. Internet sites, like Find-A-Grave, contribute greatly to this vital genealogical research tool.

Photographer's Comments: After about 10 minutes of walking through the Mattawana Cemetery, I was able to locate the large white cross on the left hand foreground, which was used to find this exact shot.

McVeytown Academy - c. 1908

SCHOOL HOUSE McVEYTOWN PA

According to a report issued in 1844, the original school, McVeytown Academy, was built of brick, fifty-two by thirty-eight feet, two stories in height, with a cupola, and with two rooms on each floor. The estimated cost was $1,750. The lot was convenient to the town, as it was already owned by the future borough. The contract was given to Ralph Bogle and carpenter Owen Thomas. The structure was completed during the school year and occupied by students in January 1845. For forty years it was the only school in the town. In 1927, the McVeytown-Oliver High School was built, with additions when Oliver Township closed its schools in the mid-1930s. In 2012, the former school also houses the McVeytown Borough offices, the Rothrock Branch of the Mifflin County Library and Snyder-Union-Mifflin Child Development Head Start.

McVeytown School House - after 1908

School House McVeytown PA

Ellis' History of Susquehanna and Juniata Valleys, notes that the settlement of what is now McVeytown was begun by Samuel Holliday in 1755. But it wasn't until 1762 that he settled in permanently and not until 1795 that the town of Waynesburg (present day McVeytown) was laid out. John McVey owned the land and was the founder of McVeytown. The town holds an annual street fair called Country Memories Day. The event is held on the Saturday of Memorial Day weekend each year. Local businesses and many artists and crafters put out stands to sell crafts and the borough's churches have charity events. The town's museum is located in the former 1845 school house, with extra displays during the Memorial Day weekend event highlighting the town's colorful history.

AROUND LEWISTOWN

Civil War Soldiers' and Sailors' Monument dedicated June 21, 1906

Monument Dedication Souvenir tumbler, 1906

Mifflin County's third county courthouse was built in 1843 and enlarged to the present size in 1878. The souvenir cup at right was issued in 1906 when the monument was dedicated. The building was extensively renovated in 2003/04 bringing the courtroom back to its former beauty. High school commencements, traveling plays and public spectacles took place in the upstairs courtroom in earlier years. Enterprises such as a butcher shop, oyster bar, an academy and various eateries occupied basement rooms at one time or another. The building currently is the home of the Mifflin County Historical Society, Juniata Valley Visitors Bureau and Chamber of Commerce, and Downtown Lewistown, Inc.

Photographer's Comments: The complete lack of power lines today on the square truly makes it much more attractive, and easier to photograph.

72   Mifflin County – THEN & NOW

Lewistown Junction – c. 1890

Postcards were popular souvenirs along the PRR.

Transport via the ubiquitous omnibus was the people-mover of choice for weary train travelers seeking a hotel bed.

In 1849, Mifflin County's link to the world was located across the Juniata River at Lewistown Junction. The railroad and telegraph office were both located at the station, vital components of communication and commerce. The Pennsylvania Historical and Museum Commission erected an Historic Marker along Rt 103 near Lewistown Junction in 1996. The station is the oldest surviving structure known to have been built by the Pennsylvania Railroad, constructed in 1848-49. On September 1, 1849, this was the scene of a banquet

Around Lewistown

celebrating the opening of the railroad to Lewistown.

Photographer's Comments: Shown shortly after the sun rose to reduce shadows for the easterly facing train station. It always amazes me that there is almost always some people there to see trains passing by. In this case, a woman and her grandson in the white car were hoping to see some trains before he was to be at school.

LEWISTOWN STATION

The oldest surviving structure known to have been built by the Pennsylvania Railroad, this station was constructed in 1848-49 as a freight handling warehouse. On September 1, 1849, this was the scene of a banquet celebrating the opening of the railroad to Lewistown. The building was renovated and converted into a passenger station in 1868.

74 *Mifflin County – THEN & NOW*

Memorial Bridge - c. 1926

MIFFLIN COUNTY BRIDGE ACROSS JUNIATA RIVER, LEWISTOWN, PA.   102008

This location, looking toward the eastern shore of the Juniata River, was the site of several transportation bridges throughout the history of Mifflin County. With the Pennsylvania Railroad station established at Lewistown Junction in 1849 on the opposite side of the river, a bridge was a must for travel and commerce. A succession of bridges crossed the Juniata River here, including: a wooden covered bridge, a steel bridge, a steel bridge with trolley tracks, later a concrete Memorial Bridge commemorating the veterans of the First World War and the present Veterans' Memorial Bridge. During the renovation of Victory Park at the Lewistown side of the bridge, a mural by artist Dwight Kirkland honors Mifflin County's many veterans from all wars (above, far right).

76 *Mifflin County – THEN & NOW*

Newly completed Memorial Bridge - 1925

Author's image - Kepler Studio Collection

Snapped by Lewistown photographer Luther F. Kepler, Sr. using a large format, 8" x 10" Kodak camera, the slow shutter speed produced the "ghost" images of a moving trolley, autos and pedestrians on the bridge. Across the river from Lewistown is the Borough of Juniata Terrace, a planned community brought into existence by the American Viscose Corporation for its workers in 1920.

Around Lewistown

Photographer's Comment: Special thanks to the tenants who allowed me to compose this shot out of their second floor bedroom window in the Ahrens Building. It was first attempted from a guest bedroom window and while close, wasn't perfect. I hesitantly asked if we could try another. They very kindly allowed me to shoot again and match up this shot.

78   *Mifflin County – THEN & NOW*

Future Site of Victory Park - c. 1914

SITE OF PUBLIC PLAYGROUND, LEWISTOWN, PA   "LET'S GET IT FINISHED."   NOLTE PHOTO.

Around Lewistown

in Burnham. Ahrens Brothers Construction Company also contracted for the enlargement of the Coleman Hotel, West Market Street (1906), the Pastime Theatre on East Market Street (1907), the Parker properties on East Market Street (now demolished) and the Reedsville Water Works.

Photographer's comments on the panorama view: As much as trees help an area look more attractive, they can sometimes hide details, in this case the Presbyterian Church Steeple while the FOE Building hides the historic courthouse clock tower.

Courtesy Jan Snedeker

The building on the corner of Juniata & West Market Streets near Victory Park was built in 1906 for the H. E. Ahrens & Brothers Construction Company. The company was based in Reading but located this office in Lewistown to take advantage of a building boom occurring in Lewistown and surrounding communities. Locally, the Company built the Wollner Building in 1906 on the southwest corner of the Square (now housing Seven Mountains Medical Center), the Sunbury & Lewistown Railroad Depot (1906) on Depot Street (now demolished), and had a "large" contract

80 *Mifflin County – THEN & NOW*

Lewistown Hotel - 1937

Author's images - Kepler Studio Collection

In the 1750s, the site was occupied by the log structure of local pioneers Arthur and Dorcas Buchanan and their family. Following Arthur's death, Dorcas Buchanan continued to live there until her death in the early 1800s. In later generations, canal traffic could be observed from the site as early as the 1830s. Across the street, warehouses buzzed with commercial activities buying and selling grains and commodities. Opened in 1937

Around Lewistown

on the corner of South Main and Water Streets, the Hotel Lewistown was considered a "fire proof" building at the time due to its steel and concrete construction. It offered accommodations at this location for 70 years before closing. However, according to a March 23, 2013 report in the Sentinel (Lewistown, PA), the old hotel may have a second life as Ansal Apartments under new owner, local businessman Joe Gagliardo.

82 *Mifflin County – THEN & NOW*

The 1856 Mifflin County Jail - c. 1935

Author's image - Kepler Studio Collection

This was the site of the county's first courthouse, a two story log building that included a courtroom on the second floor and a jail on the first. Following the log structure, a stone jail was erected and later replaced in 1856 by this building. In use for almost 145 years, a new facility was needed by the late 1990s. Phase one construction started in 1999, and was completed in December 2000, including the vehicle sally port (a secure, controlled entryway), the inmate housing area and control center, the Booking Area

Around Lewistown

and Work Release Blocks and Recreation Area. Phase two was completed in October 2001; that was the Administrative Offices, the Magisterial District Judges Office, the public lobby, the visiting area, Food Services, the medical department, multi-purpose room and inmate library. The total construction was then completed in October 2001. The first prisoners were moved into the new Mifflin County Correctional Facility on December 26, 2000. "Merry Christmas and welcome to the new jail."

84 *Mifflin County – THEN & NOW*

28   THE ELKS' HOME, LEWISTOWN, PA.

Elks Building - 1940s

E-6370

Southeast corner of Wayne and West Market Streets is the site of the Pennsylvania Railroad's district superintendent's home in the later 1900s. It was a stately home in the late Victorian style. That building was eventually used as the Elk's Orphans' Home and later replaced in the 1920s by the present structure, established as the fraternal hall of the local Elk's Club. This linen-style postcard was one

Around Lewistown

of a series highlighting other public buildings in the town. Sold by the Elk's Club in the 1990s, it was used for a short period by Mifflin County to house prisoners while the new Correctional Facility was constructed. The building is now vacant. In 2013, Elk's Lodge Number 663 is located at 229 W. 3rd Street, the former Textile Workers Union of America Hall.

Miller Theatre - Opening Night, 1949

Courtesy Paul T. Fagley

The Miller Theatre opened on April 1, 1949 and was originally a one screen movie house with over 1,200 seats, and was decorated in a handsome Art-Deco style. Among its other features was a private viewing room and a "Cry Room" where parents could take their young children to view the movie without disturbing other patrons. In 1981, the Miller was converted to a three screen multiplex, with additional screens added over the years to today's six screens. In the early 2000s, the building was recognized for its historical significance to Mifflin County.

Photographer's Comments: During the summer months, the manager of The Miller, Rob Sprankle, usually turns off the lights on the marquee to reduce bugs after the movies have started. He was kind enough to turn them back on for me without much notice… twice.

Embassy Theatre - 1938

Courtesy Friends of the Embassy

Located at 6 South Main Street is the last remaining historic theatre in Mifflin County. Opened October 17, 1927, the Embassy is an outstanding example of theatre architecture of the time period. The theatre's architecture is rare in that it resembles larger urban theatres, commonly known historically as "Broadway Picture Palaces." The original National Theatre building was built in 1916, and gutted in 1927 to be

Around Lewistown

rebuilt as the Embassy. The front facade features eclectic Colonial Revival details. It has a rectangular marquee measuring 33 feet, 6 inches, by 10 feet, 6 inches, overall. Closed since 1981, it was entered on the National Register of Historic Places in 1998 and is being restored as an operating theatre and community arts center. The theatre is owned by the Friends of the Embassy Theatre, a non-profit 501(c)(3) organization. Visit the group's web page, www.embassytheatre.org, and on Facebook, for the history and pictures of the Embassy Theatre.

90 *Mifflin County – THEN & NOW*

Coleman House - 1894

Coleman Hotel postcard showing the dining room c. 1940s

This structure was completed in 1893 following a destructive fire that razed the former Red Lion Inn, later known as the Coleman House. It was considered the newest, largest and best equipped hotel in Lewistown. Proprietor J. C. Robeson boasted that his establishment had steam heat, electric and gas lighting throughout, large simple rooms on the first floor, bus line service to all trains and complete fire protection. All this for a mere $2 per day. In 1920, John Miller purchased the property, and added a five story wing to the rear, enlarged the dining room and created a ballroom. It remained a hotel with 120 rooms when Simon and Helen Varner bought it in 1967. Acquired by the Housing Authority of Mifflin County, the Coleman underwent renovation between 1989 to 1992.

Wollner Building - c. 1940

The Wollner Building, above, during a 1950s Christmas parade, highlighting Headings Rexall Drug Store at street-level; Below, Lewistown Trust Company, c. 1920. Pallas Restaurant was a later tenant, with various offices above.

Built in 1906, the Wollner Building at 16 W. Market Street is a locally significant, turn-of-the-century commercial three-story brick structure. Its significance lies in its architecture, its connection with the urbanization of Lewistown, and its association with Calvin Greene, a prominent local businessman and founder of a banking institution (Lewistown Trust Company.) Currently, the building houses the Seven Mountains Medical Center on the first floor with private apartments on the second and third floors. Pedestrians passing the Wollner Building may notice the Greek tiles on the street-level exterior of businesses, at left.

Photographer's Comments: One of my personal favorite buildings in Lewistown.

National Hotel - c. 1894

A third story featuring a mansard-style roof with dormers was added to expand capacity. The inset shows the hotel in 1925. The building was called The Taft Hotel in later years.

In 1894, the National Hotel, on the southwest corner of South Main and Market, was considered by owner James H. Clover as "The Leading Hotel of Lewistown for Forty Years." He proclaimed his simple rooms as the "largest and best" in town. Advertised with electric lights, steam heat, modern sanitary conveniences, telephone service and location, all for

$2 per day. The horse drawn omnibus also made regular trips to Lewistown Junction. A fourth floor was added, and in a later life it was known as the Taft Hotel, by then a residential establishment, with street-level shops, including Mur Jewelry Co. at 2 West Market. A major fire halted operation. In the years before the Embassy Theatre, the original National Theatre was located on the block, and emerged from a total reconstruction in 1927 as the Embassy.

Masonic Building, 2 E. Market Street - c. 1900

In 1894, H. J. Fosnot, publisher of the Democrat & Sentinel commented, "The Masonic Temple...owned by a chartered organization known as the Masonic Association, is a creditable addition to the town. It is located on the south side of the public square. It provides a beautiful lodge room for Masonic societies... On the second floor the Don Pedro Club, a social organization, has billiard, card, reading and toilet rooms...in the rear is a cozy, well organized opera house, with a seating capacity of about eight hundred..." Purchased by John Pannizzo in 1999, the building's historic significance includes being the site of Lewistown's first post office. Artist Dwight Kirkland created a mural on the South Main Street side honoring the Logan Guards, the Civil War's First Defenders from Lewistown, PA.

98 Mifflin County – THEN & NOW

Selheimer's Hardware - c. 1912

Nolte Photo #20

Section of Sunday School Parade, Lewistown, PA. Over 1300 Participated

The location's history dates from Lewistown's founding in 1795. John Beale Selheimer and his family operated a hardware store here for decades. An 1871 article in the Lewistown *True Democrat* announced the Selheimer business as "A Magnificent Store." The hardware business continued under him until his death, when Selheimer was described as "one of the best known and prosperous merchants of the county." When newspaper magnate Henry J. Fosnot, publisher of the Lewistown *Sentinel*, purchased the building, he crowed that it was "…about the largest business deal in the history of Lewistown…" His contractor demolished the Selheimer building and constructed the current

Around Lewistown

structure in 1918. Paul F. Wilson, Sr. took ownership in 1970, and Wilson's Gifts & Jewelry has been on the corner on the Square ever since.

Photographer's Comments: This one should have been harder than it was but once you realize it's Monument Square it could only be one of two possibilities and since this is not the Wollner Building it has to be where Wilson's Jewelry is now.

100 Mifflin County – THEN & NOW

Banking Corner at Main and Brown Streets - c. 1964

The First National Bank clock was refurbished in time for Lewistown's 175th anniversary in 1970.

The **Mifflin County National Bank merged** with Citizens National Bank in 1946 and became the First National Bank, shown above in the mid-1960s at 33 E. Market. This location was known as "the banking corner" boasting the First National along with the Russell National Bank and Lewistown Trust Company, all at the intersection of Market and Brown streets.

A 1960s street directory listed businesses along that side of the block as: Berney's Toyland (31); Beacon Consumer Discount Company (29); Martha Krentzman clothing (27); Mifflin County Child Welfare (25); Weaver's Gift & Jewelery (23); Kennedy's Young Men Shop (23); A. Goldman & Son clothing (21); Penn Furniture Co.(19); Campbell's Bar & Grill (15); and Bob Davis clothing (13).

The cast-iron four faced clock was erected as early as 1905 by the Mifflin County National Bank. The timepiece ran for 13 days on one winding, a job accomplished for years by Charles P. McClure, manager

Lewistown Redevelopment

of the Mifflin County Jewelry Company located at 24 East Market. Upon his death, his son Alva W. McClure continued the service until he, too, was unable to continue due to ill health in 1967. It finally stopped running and stood mute for over a year, according to the First National Bank's Cashier John T. Connelly in 1970. Ivan Leeper, owner of a local sign company, used his resources to bring the timepiece back to life. The clock was restored in time for Lewistown's 175th anniversary in 1970. The demise of the old clock came following a collision with a delivery truck October 30, 1987. The clock base now resides in the McCoy House courtyard at 17 N. Main Street.

102 Mifflin County – THEN & NOW

McCoy House, 1938

McCoy's father was General Thomas McCoy, Mexican-American War and Civil War veteran (below). Sitting in the parlor at 17 North Main Street, above, is (left to right) his mother Margaret McCoy, sisters Margaretta McCoy, and Hannah McCoy.

McCoy House, 17 N. Main Street, Lewistown is the birth place of Frank Ross McCoy, born October 29, 1874. He was an 1897 West Point graduate, and an aide to President Theodore Roosevelt. Wounded in action at San Juan Hill in the Spanish-American War; fought the Moros in the Philippines Insurrection; Assistant to the Chief of Staff in France; commanded the "Fighting 69th" in some of the last battles of World War I;

Around Lewistown

Frank Ross McCoy (1874 - 1954) Soldier - Diplomat

Historical Marker Dedicated at 17 N. Main March 27, 1967

Chairman of the Commission of Inquiry and Conciliation (Bolivia and Paraguay) that settled the Gran Chavo War; and supervised US aid to Japan following 1923 earthquake there. He retired as a Major General in 1938 while commanding the 1st U.S. Army and II Corps Area, Governors' Island, New York. In 1939 he was President of the prestigious Foreign Policy Association and during World War II was President of the Military Commission that tried and convicted German saboteurs who landed in the United States. He died in Washington, D.C. on June 4, 1954 and was buried in Arlington National Cemetery. His wife, Frances Field Judson McCoy (1898-1973) is buried with him. The building became the museum of the Mifflin County Historical Society in 1972, and was placed on the National Register of Historic Places, 1973. It houses the General McCoy Memorial Collection donated by his widow in 1956, plus the society's other collections.

104 Mifflin County – THEN & NOW

2 E. Third Street - 1940s

LEWISTOWN MUNICIPAL BUILDING
LEWISTOWN, PA.

This site was once occupied by the Old Town Hall or city building, not to be confused with the county courthouse down the street. It was a multi-storied, brick structure housing city offices and a second floor meeting hall used by the Col. Thomas M. Hulings Post 176 of the Grand Army of the Republic, veterans of the Civil War, from 1866 to 1929. In December 1935, the Old Town Hall building was razed to make room for the new $65,000 Municipal Building. By July 1937, Lewistown's new seat of borough government was dedicated after having been constructed with the aid of Works Progress Administration funds. Construction like this, plus over 20 other public works projects in the county, helped ease local unemployment at the time. A bronze plaque by the main entrance remembers the Logan Guards, the Civil War's First Defenders from Lewistown. The library and museum of the Mifflin County Historical Society moved into the basement in 1938, and was the first home of the Gen. Frank R. McCoy Memorial collection in 1956.

106 *Mifflin County – THEN & NOW*

A Fountain Square panorama, inset left, after 1906 when Lewistown streets were brick-paved. The Valley House is visible at 151 E. Market Street. P. M. Headings pharmacy, 1909, inset right.

Fountain Square, Lewistown, Pa.

N. Dorcas & Valley Streets - Five Points - 1894

Valley, Chestnut, North and South Dorcas Streets, plus Market Street, all converge at this location. The area has been known as Five Points for well over 125 years. At the end of the 19th and into the 20th centuries a fountain and horse trough were

Around Lewistown

located in the intersection of these streets. The trough was erected in 1891, deemed a necessity for horse traffic, but was removed a few decades later. A story relates that one of Lewistown's first families, also owned one of the town's first automobiles. It was that automobile that crashed into the convenience, causing damage to car and fountain. This incident prompted a move for the watering trough's removal, since the fountain and trough posed an obstruction in the busy intersection. (The future US 322 at Lewistown passed through this intersection.) Photographs published in the 1925 *Historical Souvenir of Lewistown* featured brick paved streets at fountain square, minus the fountain, removed in the name of progress. A new community park will grace the lot nearby the fountain's former location through the Five Points/East End Neighborhood project.

108 *Mifflin County – THEN & NOW*

9 S. Dorcas Street - Sentinel Building - 1925

Built in 1910 at 9 S. Dorcas Street as the newspaper's new headquarters, the Daily Sentinel began rolling off the presses in October 1903 at its old 20 Valley Street location. The average daily circulation in 1903 was about 1,200, by 1909 it almost tripled at 3500 copies. In 2013, its 100th year in publication, subscriptions are 12,500. The Sentinel's first publisher, H. J. Fosnot & Son, also produced the Democrat & Sentinel, originally established in 1832. This building was built by George C. Tate Construction of Yeagertown, from architectural designs done by Charles Harold Lloyd of Harrisburg (1909 drawing inset left). The newspaper was published at this site until a new building was constructed in Pleasant Acres in the mid-1970's. The basement of the building was used by the Stone Arch Players for a number of their performances when it was called The Press Room Theatre. It is the site of the Salvation Army in 2012.

110 *Mifflin County – THEN & NOW*

53 Valley Street - Montgomery Carriages - c. 1875

Robert H. Montgomery, Jr. was a wagon and coach maker, with his shop located at the corner of Third and Valley Streets in the 1860s, and 70s. He started the wagon business in 1867, adding machinery for a planing mill in 1873. The manufacturing of vehicles continued at this location until 1878, when Montgomery moved to the east side of Lewistown, setting up shop opposite the Sunbury and Lewistown Railroad depot. In 1882 he added a brick works to his business. An omnibus is shown in front of his carriage shop above, a common transport for travelers to and from the railroad station.

This advertising card touts Montgomery's products as everything from buggies, carriages and spring wagons to "vehicles of every description." The advertisement has the picture of the wagon business on the front, and was donated to the Mifflin County Historical Society over fifty years ago by the family of Mrs. H. E. Best, formerly of Lewistown.

Photographer's Comments: This was one of the most difficult spots to identify

Around Lewistown

due to a lack of road signs and lack of information on the business. Because of the unique architecture and placement of the building, we were able to narrow it down to a couple of spots. At first it was thought that it could be Dorcas and Valley but that was soon eliminated. The location was then thought to either be the alley that runs from N. Dorcas to Valley and Valley or Third Street and Valley. Going from the width of the road that goes towards the horizon in the photo it is obvious that it is 3rd Street and not an alley.

112 *Mifflin County – THEN & NOW*

Woodlawn - c. 1890 (Later 200 N. Main Street)

Looking up **North Main Street** from Lewistown's Monument Square, a large stately building dominates the end of the tree lined thoroughfare. Graceful columns define the ample porches of this historic white structure. The wooded setting on the south side of Ard's Ridge is Woodlawn, once the home of Presbyterian pastor, Rev. James Sterrett Woods. Heller Hoenstine Funeral Home has been located at Woodlawn in recent times. Prior to the funeral home's occupancy, it was owned by the Borough of Lewistown, with organizations like the American Red Cross and the Boy Scouts maintaining offices there. The present day municipal parking lots, a playground, tennis courts, and the Mifflin County Library were all established on property that was originally part of Rev. James S. Woods' estate.

114 Mifflin County – THEN & NOW

2 Oak Street - City Hook & Ladder Co. - 1939/1940

City Hook and Ladder Company's second firehouse was erected in 1906 at this location. Total cost was $3,350.00. City remodeled the building in 1939 and 1940. This is the image that appeared in the 1940 program for the Fireman's Association Sate Convention held in Lewistown. A year later, City Hook and Ladder swapped buildings with the H. B. Goss Candy Company located at 317 Valley Street. Goss

Around Lewistown

moved into the old City building at 2 Oak Street, while City took over Goss' building.

The switch was instigated for a very practical reason. Robert L. Ingram of Lewistown recalled the reason given by his father, Robert J. Ingram, fire truck driver for City. On one occasion, Bob even rode beside his father in the open ladder truck, a practice likely not encouraged by his mother. It seems if a fire call came from in town, City's hook and ladder truck just dashed down Valley Street in response. If the call was out of town, maneuvering the vehicle from the firehouse and turning up Stratford's Hill became an emergency issue. Moving into the Goss building made responding to fire calls an easy turn out of the house, in either direction.

Photographer's Comments: Bob Bartlett, Captain at City Hook and Ladder was nice enough to bring out the modern engines to be photographed on a Saturday morning.

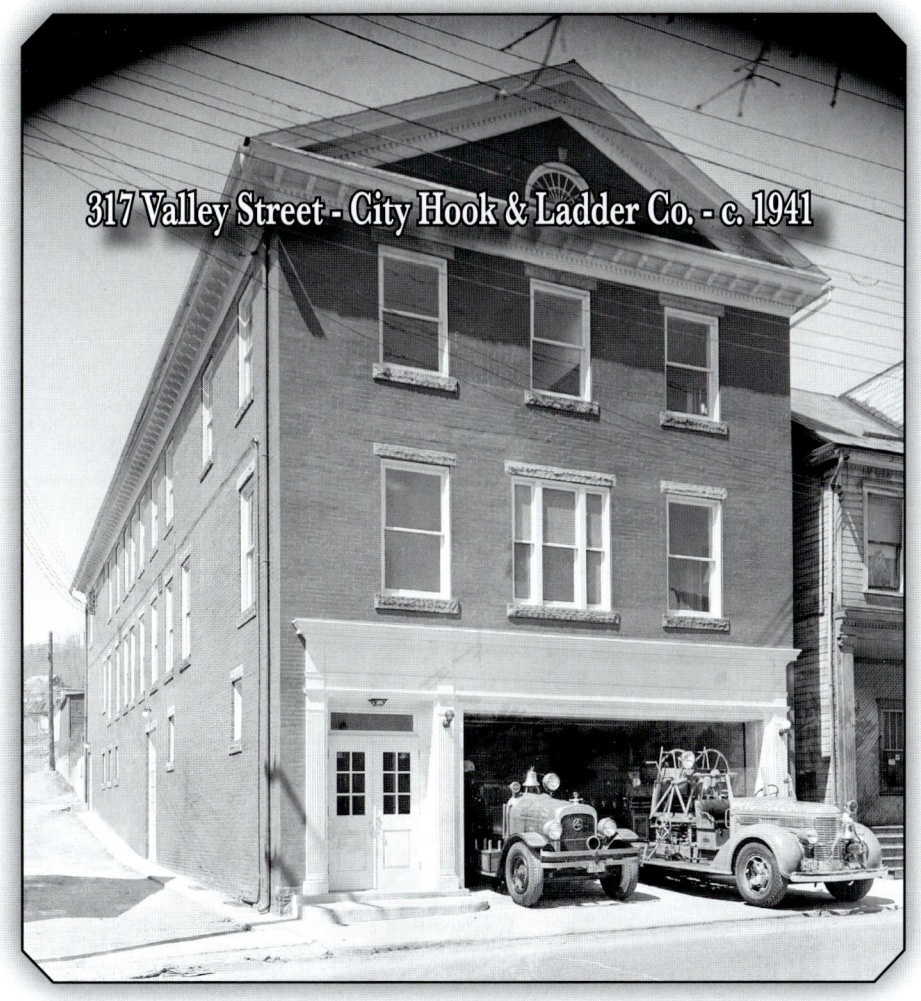

317 Valley Street - City Hook & Ladder Co. - c. 1941

Author's image - Kepler Studio Collection

116 *Mifflin County – THEN & NOW*

108 Valley Street - Fame Fire Co. - c. 1940

Fame Fire Company was one of Mifflin County's original fire companies formed in 1850 in the borough of Lewistown. Fame and Henderson Fire Company, formed in 1853, covered Lewistown Borough and surrounding communities. In 1896, Fame Fire Company records show that the assets of the organization were $28.00. The company purchased an American LaFrance 500 gallon steam fire en-

Around Lewistown

22 W. Third St. - Henderson Fire Co. - 1940

gine and a new hose cart at a cost of $39.00. All these were pulled to the fire scene by firemen. In 1938 a 1000-gallon capacity Ahren-Fox pumper was purchased with all necessary equipment at a cost of $15,000.00. In 1923, Fame first started transporting patients in a donated hearse, increasing its ambulance capacity over time. In January of 1994, Fame Emergency Medical Service moved out of the fire station and into it's new and current building at 701 Valley Street. The Fame building at 108 Valley Street is now closed.

Henderson organized in December 1853 as Henderson Hose, Hook and Ladder Company, named for it founder, Dr. Joseph Henderson. He was a regimental commander in the War of 1812 and Mifflin County's member of Congress from 1832-1836. The fire house was located at 22 W. Third Street. In 1898 a hand cart was purchased and two years later the fire house was equipped with a fire bell, which previously hung in the bell tower of the historic courthouse, according to the Company's history in the 1940 program of the Firemen's Association State Convention held in Lewistown. Fire fighting services formerly of Fame and Henderson merged to form United Fire Company at the Third Street location.

Photographer's Comments: The firemen at the United Company, which occupies the old Henderson Firehouse site, were kind enough to pull out their trucks to replicate this shot.

218 S. Main Street - Brooklyn Fire Co., c. 1925

Brooklyn Firehouse

1924 - A new 1000-gallon pumper cost $13,688. Almost $9,000 was borrowed and paid off in two years.

A tough little fire company mascot, King, came to the Brooklyn in 1916. He served as mascot for many years and died at age 19.

Courtesy Genevieve Gregg McCardle

The Brooklyn Hose Company was organized April 12, 1897 in a shoemaker's shop in Lewistown's Sixth Ward by two shoemakers George Temple and John Morrison. A hand-drawn cart was the company's first fire-fighting apparatus purchased by the Borough. This building is on the former Brannon property on South Main Street, purchased by Brooklyn in 1927 for $10,000.00. An architectural firm of

Hodge & Hill of Philadelphia drew up the plans and supervised construction, which cost $39,670.00. Structures on either side were purchased over time allowing for expansion at what is 218 South Main in 2012.

Photographer's Comments: The firemen at the Brooklyn Fire Company were nice enough to pull out a couple of trucks to help replicate the original photo.

120 *Mifflin County – THEN & NOW*

900 S. Main Street - Green Gables Hotel - 1933

Sun porch, Green Gables - 1931

Courtesy Christeena Kearns

On July 9, 1931, as the Great Depression deepened, Green Gables Hotel opened, with owner Obed O. Orner, announcing that his hostelry offered 22 guest rooms to accommodate travelers and locals alike. Orner was reported in the Sentinel (Lewistown, PA) to declare

Around Lewistown

that the structure cost $100,000 in renovation costs of a former barn. The hotel postcard above was sent to Germany in 1933 by a young German seeking employment in the United States. He wrote to his mother in the Rhineland district, commenting that the Juniata Valley reminded him of home. The postcard was purchased through an on-line auction in 2010. The seller was located in Germany, so this little glimpse of history survived the Second World War only to be retrieved almost 70 years later from where it originated.

S. B. Peters & Son - c. 1913

Courtesy Linda Howell O'Dell

The S. B. Peters & Son store and residence was located at 3 W. Hale Street, Lewistown. Solomon B. Peters died at his home on June 9, 1933 at the age of 78. He was one of Lewistown's few remaining canal boatmen at the time of his death. For 68 years he had been a resident of Lewistown, first working for the canal company as a boatman and later being employed for 25 years by Standard Steel Works. In 1909 he entered the grocery business with his son, Charles E. Peters, who continued the business, at the corner of S.

Main and W. Hale Streets, under the firm name of S.B. Peters and Son. Peters retired from active participation in the business about 1901. The donor stated that the back portion of the house held the office of WKVA radio and that the local high school cross-county football rivalry trophy, known as the "Old Iron Kettle," came from the basement of the radio office. In 2012, the nearby Kish Apartments at 196 South Main Street is an independent living community.

124 Mifflin County – THEN & NOW

Mifflin County Library - 1942

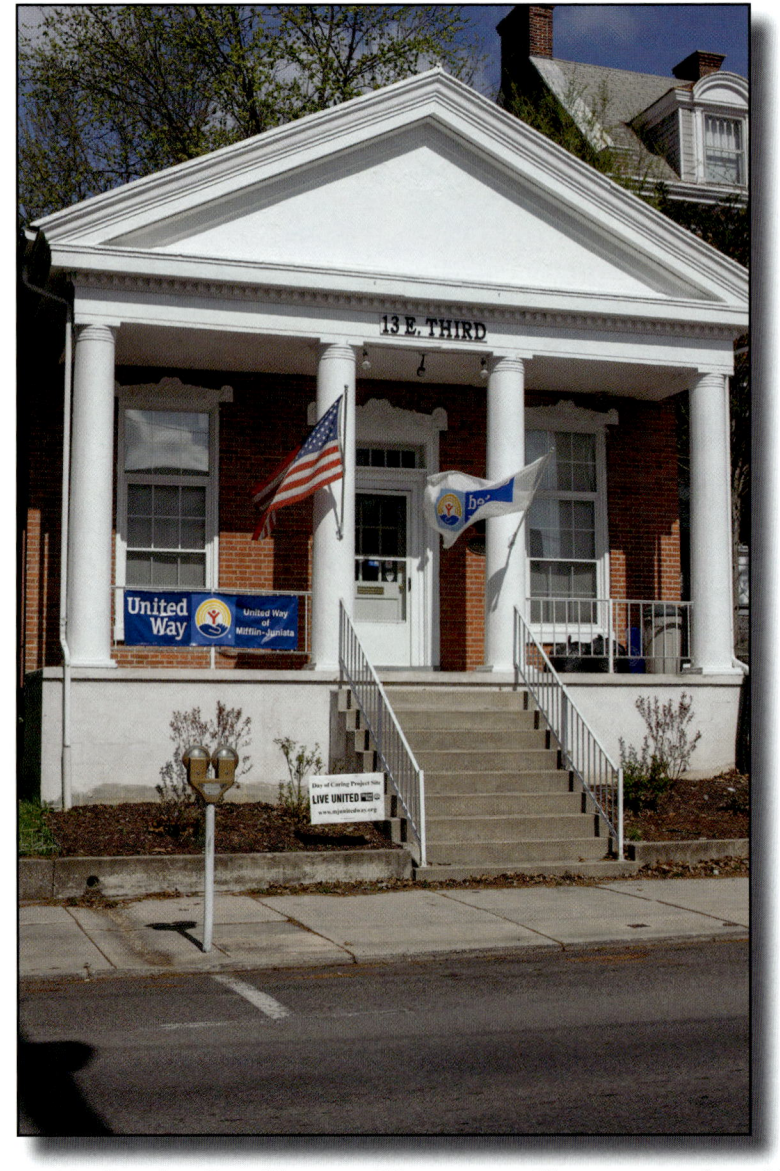

The Apprentices' Literary Society or ALS Building at 13 East Third Street was built in 1853, and occupied by that organization until 1911. At that time, the Lewistown Public Library acquired the building reopening in January 1942 as the Mifflin County Library, a county-wide free lending library. The county library moved to 25 South Brown Street in 1955, and later to the current facility near Woodlawn. In 2012, the United Way of Mifflin-Juniata occupies the historic structure, one of Lewistown's classic 19th century buildings.

Around Lewistown

ST. JOHN'S EVANGELICAL CHURCH, 3RD AND MAIN STS., LEWISTOWN, PA.
Jos. S. Waream. Beautiful Lewistown and Vicinity

St. John's Lutheran Church - c. 1902

Lewistown's first Lutheran congregation formed in 1798, and its first church structure, built in 1824, was located where the United Fire and Rescue Services at 22 W. Third Street is in 2012. The congregation purchased this lot in 1850, but the church erected there burned before completion in 1852. It was rebuilt and dedicated in 1853. There have been additions and extensions to the present building at 120 North Main Street in 1911 and 1919. In 1965, the Christian Education Building was added to the west end of the building. A major renovation of the old chapel and extensions was completed in 1993. The structure and location are recognized for its historical significance.

126 *Mifflin County – THEN & NOW*

Sacred Heart of Jesus Roman Catholic Church - postcard c. 1909

Jos. S. Waream, Beautiful Lewistown and Vicinity SACRED HEART CATHOLIC CHURCH, LEWISTOWN, PA. 7345

By 1827, the Catholic population grew to the point that a priest was appointed to Lewistown. The church web site notes: *This parish was founded in 1830, when a chapel was built on the present site, and then blessed by Bishop Francis P. Kenrick of Philadelphia, Pa., the diocese to which Lewistown then belonged. Catholics had been served as early as 1798 by a missionary priest stationed at Conewago. The current church build-*

ing (corner of North Dorcas and East Third Streets) was constructed in 1922. The Sacred Heart School (SHS) is at 110 North Dorcas. The school and church website also explains that SHS began with a kindergarten for the fall term, September 1948. Parishioners paid a monthly $2 tuition, $6 for non-parishioners. Today's parish school, 78 students in grades K-5, was erected in 1954 by Monsignor Owen F. Reilly. The church cemetery is located adjacent to the school.

128   Mifflin County – THEN & NOW

New Presbyterian Church, Lewistown, Pa.

17 E. Third Street - Presbyterian Church - 1910

On this site at 17 East Third Street, a stone church was erected in 1820 and was torn down in 1854 to make room for a larger brick church. That church, in turn, was replaced by the present structure. In 1905, one member offered to be one of 10 to give $1,000 to build a new church and it was voted to build "a new church and chapel, one or both, on the lot now occupied…" It was completed in

Around Lewistown

1910 at a cost of $50,000. In recent times, an elevator was added on the Third Street side. The church was recognized for its historic significance, including that a Presbyterian congregation was formed in Lewistown about one year after Mifflin County was established in 1789. Since there was no building at that early time, church meetings were held outdoors or in the county's first log courthouse.

LEWISTOWN REDEVELOPMENT

A collection of photographs from the late J. Martin Stroup was donated to the Mifflin County Historical Society after his death in the 1970s. Stroup was editor of the Sentinel (Lewistown, PA), past president of the Mifflin County Historical Society and a tireless local historian who put his camera to good use. Included in his collection were images of Lewistown just prior to downtown redevelopment of the late 1960s and early 1970s. As with any town or

131

Lewistown's 175th anniversary in 1970 offered hope for a prosperous future. A souvenir booklet (opposite) revealed the architect's concept that city fathers believed would help the borough grow. Admittedly an ambitious project, the concept envisioned the ultimate in downtown shopping convenience — architecturally symmetrical buildings adjoining a tree lined mall and spacious parking facilities.

village in the county, the passage of just a few weeks, months or years can change the landscape. A new road, a fire or construction on an empty lot seems to erase a fragment of our collective memory. The cliché "Out of sight, out of mind" might just apply. It is through photographs that we can recall and begin to understand what preceded us. Stroup's photographs tease those of a certain age with thoughts of Lewistown in the 1960s. Nathaniel Thierwechter's contemporary images record today's reality for the next generation.

132 *Mifflin County – THEN & NOW*

Downtown Businesses Aid Lot Development

THE SENTINEL
Established Oct. 10, 1903 LEWISTOWN, PA., SATURDAY, APRIL 29, 1967

See Demolition Of Properties Ended by April 1

Will Provide 400 Parking Places:
Parking Authority Inks Redevelopment Papers

Giving Credit Where It's Due
EDITORIAL

Urban Renewal Supported By Business Community

Clear the old to make room for the new. Demolition photographs in the redevelopment area, are clockwise from left, McMeen's Department Store; East Third Street residences viewed from the alley with First Baptist Church at 11 E. Third in background and looking toward the new Bon Ton building (former E. E. McMeen) open for business at 111-121 E. Market Street.   Ner B. Goss,

Lewistown Redevelopment

133

Courtesy Trolley Car Café

former member of Borough Council and long-time proponent of urban renewal, became executive director of the Mifflin County Redevelopment Authority in the mid-1960s. Organization of the authority was the first step in the project. Goss was assisted by Walter G. Reed, Jr., Relocation Director and JoAnn Shoemaker, Secretary. Other authority members included: Randall H. Knepp, chairman; Robert M. Welham, vice-chairman; Joseph B. Eisenhart, Jr., Richard C. Noerr and Charles (Ken) Wagner. Relocation was followed by three phases of demolition prior to new structures going up. The Bon Ton, Joe Katz and Hugh B. McMeen were the first retailers to reopen on E. Market and N. Brown Streets.

134 Mifflin County – THEN & NOW

West side North Dorcas Street from East Third Street to the alley

Stately homes lined the upper west side of North Dorcas Street, including the Methodist parsonage at No. 32, extreme right, (full view, inset) and the James A. Kepler property, No. 30, that also housed

Lewistown Redevelopment

the Kepler Studio. The photographic business, formerly at 127 East Market, moved to this location prior to the death of founding partner, Luther F. Kepler, Sr. In addition, the Lewistown YMCA was next door at 14 N. Dorcas.

Photographer's Comments: Being born well after Redevelopment some of these locations were difficult to pin point. Luckily many long time Lewistown residents were more than happy to help me locate these spots.

West side of North Dorcas Street from Five Points to East Third Street

The Lewistown YMCA was at 14 North Dorcas Street. The cornerstone was set September 8, 1918, as construction continued through 1919 until July 1920, when the building was dedicated and open to the public followed by a community dinner.

The building featured a swimming pool, gymnasium, recreation rooms and accommodations for overnight guests. In May 1920, Rev. Reid S. Dickson purchased what was called "Scout Field," and donated it to the YMCA for outdoor sports and a playground. Later that area would be called Dickson Field and in 2013 is Lewistown's Rec Park.

During the Second World War Lewistown's United Service Organizations (USO) servicemen's center was located at the YMCA. The USO offered a friendly greeting from female volunteers and good food for the many traveling servicemen passing through while on leave, or heading to assignments.

The Lewistown and Burn-

Lewistown Redevelopment

ham YMCA organizations merged shortly before the redevelopment project began the demolition phase. Other addresses on this side of the street in the mid-1960s included: the Selective Service Board (4); Mary Harris Beauty Salon (6); J. T. Hays and Virginia Kumpf (8). In 2012, a business center and a parking plaza occupy this section of North Dorcas.

138 *Mifflin County – THEN & NOW*

I.O.O.F. Building, 1909

West side South Dorcas Street from Five Points to East Water Street

Danks & Company held this corner of South Dorcas and Market Streets for generations in what was originally the International Order of Odd Fellows Hall (IOOF). In 1967, Danks

Lewistown Redevelopment 139

signed the first private developer contract, and a loan and grant contract was executed with the Federal Government (Dept. of Housing and Urban Development) assuring funds for the project. A statement published in Lewistown's 175th Anniversary History in 1970, recalled, "Demolition, which must occur before new structures can be erected, began in 1968 when several buildings on South Dorcas Street...were torn down."

140 *Mifflin County – THEN & NOW*

South side of East Market Street from Five Points to Brown Street

Lewistown Redevelopment

At left is East Market Street as many still recall this portion of Lewistown's business district. From Five Points east to Brown Street, starting at Danks & Co. Department Store at No. 152, the following occupied this side of the block in 1964: Danks Men's Shop (148); F. W. Woolworth Co. Department Store (144-146); Rea & Derick Drug Store (136); Budget Plan Consumer Discount Co. and P. S. Foss Jewelery (134); Schulman's Clothing (130); Bargaintown Vitamin Discount (124); B.E. Nicodemus, physician (116); Tom Johnson Shoe Store (112); J.S. Raub Shoe Store (108); Princess Shop Clothing (106); F. M. Wian, Dentist (104 1/2); Wian Shoe Store (104); Lewistown Trust Company and law offices of C. R. Whitehill (102).

142 Mifflin County – THEN & NOW

IOOF Building, 152 E. Market, c. 1920s

DANKS & CO. George H. Danks was a dry goods merchant in Tioga County, PA prior to arriving in Mifflin County after 1920. In the 1929 Street Directory of Lewistown, his prosperous store was located at 152 East Market Street.

Danks c. 1960

The Danks family has deep family roots around or near the village of Southeast in Putnam County, New York. Through US Census records, this lower Hudson Valley settlement was home to Eli Dancks (Danks) and family, grandfather of company founder, George H. Danks (1866 or 67 - 1931).

George's father, Amos Danks and his wife Sarah, are listed there in the Census of 1860; his occupation, shoemaker.

Amos joined the Union Army in 1862, and served with the 172 NY Vol. Infantry, later transferred to NY Vol., 6th Heavy Artillery, Co. I, as a Private. By 1870, his occupation was halter, one who makes bridles and halters for cattle or horses.

George H. Danks and wife Ruth Hathaway Danks married in 1894. The couple, with children Esther, Eugene and Sarah

Lewistown Redevelopment

The Danks Building by Daniel Rowe Stratford, Lemoyne, PA, c. 1970

Jane, resided in Knoxville and Westfield, both towns in Tioga County, Pennsylvania in 1910 and 1920, respectively. Esther died prior to 1920. In each location, George's occupation is noted as dry goods merchant. The family came to Lewistown in the 1920s.

Daughter Sarah Jane Danks (1906-1966) married Harry Alvin Robinson (1900-1971), who later followed as Danks & Co. president after George's passing in 1931. The Robinsons had two daughters, Mrs. Richard (Anne) Conklin and Mrs. Robert (Susan) Welham. Both Richard and Robert joined the company in later years. Robinson lead Danks through its greatest expansion, according to the Lewistown Sentinel at the time of his death, at one time operating a chain of five stores across central and eastern Pennsylvania. Robert Welham joined the company in 1955. He recalled the property pictured in the architectural drawing, c. 1960, opposite:

We rented the corner property from the Odd Fellow's Lodge, and operated a men's store on the corner of Market & Dorcas across the street. We bought the building next to the corner, which was formerly a G. C. Murphy Store. We moved the men's store over to this property, as well as several departments from the corner property. We finally convinced the Odd Fellows to allow us to knock holes through the walls to make us all one store. It was then that we remodeled the property as shown in the drawing.

144 *Mifflin County – THEN & NOW*

Courtesy W. Jaynee Carolus

West side of South Dorcas Street from the alley to Water Street

From the alley behind the Danks Building, South Dorcas Street continued to Water Street. The former Mann Edge Tool Company office building can be seen at extreme left (full view, inset).

Lewistown Redevelopment

Other 1964 occupants of this block include: IOOF hall (2); R. W. Wagner Co., printing (6); Oscar F. Brush, Justice of the Peace (8); Margaret M. Tussey (10); James Leoras (12); Kate S. Thrush (18); W. A. DeVerter, Accountant ((22); Leoras Restaurant (26-28); Mifflin County Youth Guidance Council, Mifflin County Domestic Relations and Mifflin County Probation (28).

146 *Mifflin County – THEN & NOW*

West side of South Dorcas Street from alley to Five Points

Oscar F. Brush's Justice of the Peace office is listed as No. 8 in the 1964 street directory of Lewistown. Nearby, parked curb-side, is an emergency vehicle, down the street from the Danks

Lewistown Redevelopment

Building and the Odd Fellow's Hall. Just prior to demolition, some of the buildings were unsecured. A look around the veteran JP's empty office - a place where pleadings were heard, fines assessed and notarized documents issued - was a scattering of crumpled, blank legal forms littering the floor. In a corner was a tattered book, *Man & the Motor Car*. Dated 1936, the discard bears the stamp, "O. F. Brush, Justice of the Peace - My Commission Expires First Monday in January, 1938." (See inset at left.)

West side of South Dorcas Street from Water Street to Five Points

The popular Leoras Restaurant (26-28), shown in the inset, was a hit with locals and travelers alike. The eatery closed here in mid-1968 prior to demolition and relocated to South Brown Street. The building at the left on the corner of South Dorcas and Water Streets, was once the Davis House, one of

Lewistown Redevelopment 149

Lewistown's many 19th century hotels. In a photo of the hotel appearing in *Images of America - Mifflin County*, the windows and sills, plus the roof line are easily recognizable.

One of the features of the 1970s redevelopment plan for Lewistown was to have ample, tree-lined, off-street parking for the shopping public, shown above in 2012.

150 *Mifflin County – THEN & NOW*

North side of East Market Street from Brown Street to Five Points

The north side of East Market held many memorable shopping experiences. The 1964 Lewistown Street Directory lists, starting at the intersection of Market and Brown Streets, J. B. Katz, Inc. clothing business at No. 101, followed by: Marrone's Foodtown Market (107); E. E. McMeen Co. Department Store (111-

Lewistown Redevelopment   151

The Bon Ton - 1970

121); H. B. McMeen & Son Furniture (129); Pennsylvania Department of Health (133); Prep Shop Clothing, Ruhl's Clothing and T. M. VanNatta, Optometrist (135); Friendship Book Store (137); Betty's Alterations and Watchmaker J. W. Warholak (139); Kauffman's Music & Furniture (143-145); Household Finance Consumer Discount (151). The Bon Ton in 2012 is the business descendant of the E. E. McMeen Co. Department Store.

152   *Mifflin County – THEN & NOW*

The Smith Bros. Building at 151 E. Market replaced the much earlier Valley House hotel that dated from the 19th century. The Harrisburg Telegraph had offices there in the 1930s.

The former Smith Building on the corner; Kauffman's Music and Furniture Store is two doors down. The redevelopment project noted that the Lewistown project was unique, citing that at the time, it was the first community in the country to attack the problem of deteriorating buildings "from the center out," rather than modernizing "from the outside in."

North side of East Market Street from Five Points to Brown Street

Lewistown Redevelopment 153

By late 1969 and into 1970, workmen completed new buildings for Paul S. Foss Jewelers, Tom Johnson Shoes, and additional spaces to be rented by the developers. Eventually Kauffman's Music and Furniture Store was completed, the store local high school band students patronized for instrument supplies. In 2012, the former Kauffman's location is occupied by Capperella Furniture. (145 E. Market)

East Third Street from North Dorcas Street to North Brown Street

As plans for redevelopment moved forward, one of the pressing issues was ample parking for shoppers. The Downtown Merchant's Association pledged to make a $25,000 to $30,000 cash contribution toward the building of two parking plazas. One was proposed to be off East Third Street, and another on West Third with access to Monument Square and Market

Street. Fifty-eight downtown merchants, and business and professionals along Market, Brown, Main and Wayne streets contributed $12,685 for parking in September 1967. Cost of the two lots was projected at $112,000, with nickel meters in each. These lots, plus enlarging the Water Street Central Plaza, would provide 400 spaces for downtown parking.

156 *Mifflin County – THEN & NOW*

Intersection of North Brown and East Third Streets

The south side of East Third Street (between North Dorcas and North Brown Streets) was generally lined with private residences, owned or rented. A portion of the block would provide parking for Market Street stores like the McMeen's Department Store, soon to be merged with the Bon Ton, Kauffman's Music and Furniture, or the various banks.

D. E. Smith, Mifflintown contractor, demolished the houses as

Lewistown Redevelopment

well as the old Farmer's Market at 10 W. Third and the former Novak Garage building at 12-20 W. Third, earlier Keystone Motor Co. Middlecreek Construction Company graded and paved the lots at a low bid of $65,770, while the H. B. McMeen estate sold the property to the Parking Authority for $65,770, according to Sentinel reports, dated September 20, 1967.

East side of North Brown Street from East Third Street

North Brown Street mid-1960s occupants listed as: Verna S. Bair at No. 33; Harry S. Berlin, dentist (29-31); S. C. Sivitz, podiatrist (27); Dale Hindeman (25); Claire S. Rupp (23); R. S. Welsh, insurance (21);

Lewistown Redevelopment

Mifflin County Saving & Loan Assn., E. W. Feldman, dentist, Ruth V. Hill (19); L. V. Rhodes, optometrist (17); Mabel J. Berryman (15); Marie G. McGonigal, dressmaker (5). In 2012, AAA Central Penn is located at No. 33 N. Brown, others include: Wright Associates (27); Michael T. Goss, DDS, general dentistry (23); MCS Bank, main office (19); and Sacred Heart of Jesus Roman Catholic Church parish office (9).

160 *Mifflin County – THEN & NOW*

Jos. Katz & Co., 1909

East side of North Brown Street from East Market Street intersection

Some of the businesses that first moved to new buildings in 1970 were H. B. McMeen and Joe Katz Clothing. Katz occupied its former spot, 101 E. Market. Hugh B. McMeen & Son, furniture

Lewistown Redevelopment

H. B. McMeen - 1970

Joe Katz - 1970

and accessories, was located at 129 East Market, and opened in a new store at 9 North Brown. Sacred Heart of Jesus Roman Catholic Church parish office is there in 2012. Two financial institutions comprise the banking corner in 2012. MCS Bank Loan Center is at 101, above, while First National Bank, in the former Russell Bank building, sits diagonally across the intersection at 32 East Market.

Southeast corner of South Brown Street and East Market Street

Lewistown Trust Co. and Charles R. Whitehill, Attorney-at-law were listed in 1964 at No. 102 E. Market Street.

On South Brown Street: Dutch's Diner (9-11); Plaidland Storage, Civil Defense, Empire School of Beauty and rear, Plaidland Trading Stamps showroom (19); T. B. Haffley (21); Jane W. Sherman (23); V. R. Harbst (25); Alice R. Dippery (27); Mifflin County Li-

Lewistown Redevelopment

brary and Mifflin County Superintendent of Schools (35). The Trust Company remained at its banking corner location but was merged with the Juniata Valley Bank in 1998. The building transitioned from bank to presently Service Access & Management, Inc.

Photographer's Comments: This was slightly difficult to locate as this gorgeous building hasn't been around for a long time.

164 *Mifflin County – THEN & NOW*

Dutch's Diner, 9-11 S. Brown

East side of South Brown Street

The former drive-thru for the Trust Company, later the Juniata Valley Bank, is used for parking in 2012. One of the Trust Company's long-time employees, Styron Reichenbach, was well known as an

Lewistown Redevelopment

amateur photographer, annually sending photo Christmas cards featuring Lewistown scenes. Upon his passing, the bank added a memorial garden and plaque in the area of the drive-thru window where bank patrons could enjoy seasonal flowers. Since the bank closed, the plaque (inset above) was donated to the Mifflin County Historical Society, plus numerous photographs snapped by Reichenbach.

166 Mifflin County – THEN & NOW

Intersection of South Brown and East Water Streets

Mifflin County Library, 35 S. Brown

The tracks that traverse Water Street once carried rail traffic of the Sunbury & Lewistown Branch of the Pennsylvania Railroad. In 2012, this section is part of 11 miles of track operated by the Juniata Valley Railroad. Incorporated in 1996, JVRR assumed the Conrail operation of the three branch lines radiating out of Lewistown.

The former Mifflin County Library at 35 South Brown Street was filled to capacity. Books were stacked in

Lewistown Redevelopment

the aisles and around the shelves when the much needed move was made to the present modern building at 123 N. Wayne Street, near Woodlawn. Private developers subsequently signed contracts with the remaining businesses for completion of the initial phases of redevelopment. The Sentinel reported that the original project encompassed 12.7 acres. Upon completion of this area, the comprehensive plan then called for "spot" redevelopment throughout the business district, as Lewistown "continues to look to the future while being proud of its heritage."

168   *Mifflin County – THEN & NOW*

Aerial view of Lewistown, PA, c. 1950-51

Lewistown Redevelopment 169

Aerial View, Lewistown, PA, April 10, 2013 - Monument Square and Historic Courthouse (upper left); Five Points (mid-right); Streets include: Main (left); Brown (center) and Dorcas Street (right); W & E Water Street, parallel to Kishacoquilas Creek. - Photo by Sara Buffington

Behind the Aerial Shot

Scotland's national poet, Robert Burns, wrote in 1785, "The best-laid schemes o' mice an' men/Gang aft agley." The last portion in Burns' Scots dialect popularly translates "often go astray." Fact is, plans can become quite bumpy now and then. Our plans did.

Lewistown businessman, Mike Buffington, agreed to fly project photographer, Nathaniel Thierwechter, over Lewistown in a Cessna 150F to capture a modern aerial view of town. The arrangements were made, and both met at Mifflin County Airport, Reedsville for the auspicious flight.

Only problem was that Nathaniel's long legs just would not fit into the passenger space, no matter what adjustments were made to the accommodations!

On to Plan B. Mike's wife, Sara, agreed to take to the air with her husband and collect the image for us. The aerial photo was taken on April 10, 2013.

Mike explained, "Noah is normally my co-pilot on most of my flights around central Pennsylvania and loves taking aerial photos, but at his age he normally is just using a point and shoot camera…"

Sara, Mike noted, is not afraid of flying at all, but quite prone to motion sickness. The day they flew to take this aerial photo was not very smooth, Mike remembered, recalling "she definitely had enough by the time we returned to the airport."

☞ Sara and Mike Buffington, with son Noah, at the Mifflin County Airport, Reedsville. Sara snapped the aerial view of Lewistown, page 169, with husband Mike at the controls of a 1966 Cessna 150F. The plane is owned by the Mifflin County Flying Club Inc., a non-profit organization, formed the end of 2010 by Buffington and several others. Their goal is to keep an airplane at the Mifflin County Airport available for students and others to use. The club has seven active members in 2013, either private or student pilots. To learn more about the club visit: www.mcflyingclub.info

After Thoughts

OLD MAPS & DISCOVERIES

One of the most useful tools for researching building locations over time is a collection of graphic, color-coded maps known as the Sanborn Fire Insurance Maps™.

They are a highly useful resource for historical research, planning, preservation, genealogical research, sociological studies and research of urban geography. The Mifflin County Historical Society holds a collection of Lewistown maps for the years 1904, 1910 and 1928. The '28 version has revisions added up to 1949.

The maps were originally created for assessing fire insurance liability in urbanized areas in the United States. The Sanborn maps themselves are large-scale lithographed street plans at a scale of 50 feet to one inch (1:600) on 21 inch by 25 inch sheets of paper formed into volumes.

These collections contain an enormous amount of information, and include outlines of each building and outbuilding, the location of windows and doors, street names, street and sidewalk widths, property boundaries, fire walls, natural features (rivers, canals, etc.), railroad corridors and much more.

Historical research is the most obvious use, however, genealogists use

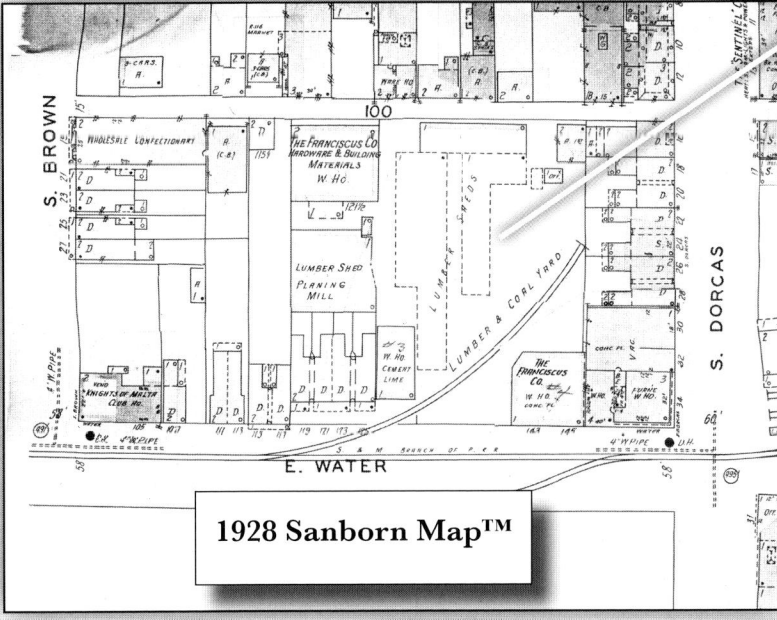

1928 Sanborn Map™

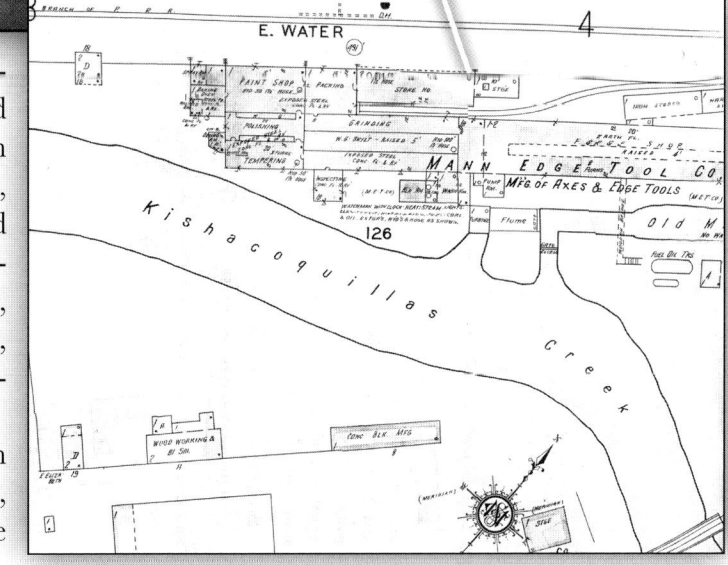

172 Mifflin County – THEN & NOW

the maps to locate the residences and workplaces of ancestors. In this case, the Sanborn maps identified the numerous industrial-type buildings and rail spur located south of the alley extending to Water Street.

Researching this book inspired many nostalgic conversations with those who experienced life in a particular neighborhood. The aerial view of Lewistown on page 168 generated much discussion. It was shared by Doug and Marsha Wagner of the The Trolley Car Café, where the photo is on permanent display.

One who knew this part of town like the proverbial "back of his hand" was William H. "Bill" Logan, Jr. His father, William Sr. and his uncle, Steve Leoras, opened a restaurant at 26-28 South Dorcas. The eatery relocated during redevelopment. In November 1968, Leoras Cafeteria opened in the basement of 19 S. Brown Street. Nephew Bill Logan bought the business in 1977, with Aunt Phoebe Leoras working there into the 1990s. Bill sold out in 2001.

His recollections include:

The aerial photo was taken in 1950 or 1951. The building at 19 South Brown was remodeled and added to starting in 1949. The VFW bought the lot on Water Street that came up behind the old candy company building. Lot number 111 and 113 on your old map (Sanborn Map). *You can see from the aerial photo that the concrete driveway was new. My father owned 26 and 28 South Dorcas Street. When my Uncle Steve (Leoras) came home from Europe in 1946, they decided to put a restaurant in that building. I can remember Franciscus Lumber yard being out the back door of the restaurant. Beside the restaurant was Yearick's Dray office. Then the big red brick on the corner (former Davis House) was where Stoicheff's lived and had their auto parts business.*

Bill concluded, "Thanks for the memories!"

1885 Sanborn Map™ of Lewistown, at right, gives an illustrative view of Five Points, and F. G. Franciscus Hardware, almost 70 years before the 1951 aerial photograph. - Courtesy Digital Map Drawer, Penn State University Libraries

Bibliography

Atlas of Perry, Juniata and Mifflin Counties, Pennsylvania. Philadelphia: Pomeroy, Whitman & Co. 1877.

Blardone, Chuck ed., *Lewistown and the Pennsylvania Railroad - From Moccasins to Steel Wheels.* Altoona, PA Pennsylvania Railroad Technical & Historical Society, 2000.

Chamber of Commerce, Mifflin County Development Committee, *A Survey of the Resources and Opportunities of Mifflin County, Pennsylvania.* Harrisburg, PA: Archives Publishing Company of Pennsylvania, 1947.

Convention Program of the Firemen's Association of the State of Pennsylvania. Lewistown, Pa., 1940.

Golden Jubilee, 1911-1961 - Burnham Pennsylvania - Historical Book. Burnham, PA, 1961.

Ellis, Franklin. *History of that part of the Susquehanna and Juniata Valleys, Embraced in the Counties of Mifflin, Juniata, Perry, Union and Snyder in the Commonwealth of Pennsylvania.* Philadelphia: Everts, Peck and Richard, 1886.

Elliott, Richard Smith. *Notes Taken in Sixty Years.* St. Louis, MO: R. P. Studley & Co., Printers, 1883.

Fosnot, H. J. *Lewistown, Penna., As It Is.* Lewistown, PA: The *Lewistown Gazette*, 1894.
— *Lewistown - The Gem of the Juniata Valley.* Lewistown, PA: The Sentinel Printing & Publishing House, 1909.

Housing Authority of the County of Mifflin. *The Coleman House.* Lewistown, PA: Housing Authority, 1992.

Lewistown Old and New. Lewistown, PA: Bell Telephone Co. of Penna., 1930.

Mifflin County Historical Society Research Library archives:
— *Democrat & Sentinel* (Lewistown, PA): July 22, 1909.
— *Sentinel* (Lewistown, PA): March, April, May, September 1967; March 1969
— *Lewistown, Pennsylvania Street Directory.* 1902, 1938, 1964

Mifflin County Historical Society. *Two Hundred Years - A Chronological List of Events in the History of Mifflin County, Pennsylvania 1752 - 1957.* Lewistown, PA: Mifflin County Historical Society, 1957.

Sentinel Company. *Historical Souvenir of Lewistown, Penna.* Lewistown, PA: The Sentinel Company and Old Home Week Celebration Committee, 1925.

Sentinel (Lewistown, PA). *Climb Aboard! Celebrate Historic Mifflin County.* Lewistown, PA: The Sentinel Company, 1989.

Shively, R. H., ed. *Commemorative Biographical Encyclopedia of the Juniata Valley, comprising the Counties of Huntingdon, Mifflin, Juniata and Perry, Pennsylvania.* Chambersburg, PA: J. M. Runk & Co., 1897.

Souvenir Booklet on the History of Lewistown, Pennsylvania and the Greater Lewistown Area. Quasquisesquicentennial of Lewistown, Pa. 1795-1970. Lewistown, PA, 1970.

Stroup, J. M. & Bell, R.M. *The Genesis of Mifflin County, Pennsylvania.* Lewistown, PA: Mifflin County Historical Society, 1958.

Grand Street, c. 1914 & 2012

Is preserving the past important to you? If so, here's how you can help.

Consider this? There are thousands of photo postcards, photographs and snapshots filed in shoe boxes or albums tucked away in closets and attics across the area. This wealth of vintage images illustrating Mifflin County's vanishing past represents a trove of historic treasures.

Many are photo postcards, but it's just such images that often depict a bygone era in a most appealing way. Every year individuals donate such photos to the Mifflin County Historical Society, some are used in this book or in other society publications. Even if not immediately published, such images are digitally preserved for future generations.

If donating is not your choice, a digital scan of an image can be accomplished at the society office, without any harm to your family photos, and returned while you're waiting.

Another option, if you are technologically equipped, would be to scan the image yourself at a high resolution (360 dpi or larger) and donating your digital scan. Email the society at **info@mifflincountyhistoricalsociety.org**

Please contact the historical society at 242-1022 during regular hours, Tuesday or Wednesday from 10 - 4 to make arrangements to have your photo scanned. Thank you!

Mifflin County Historical Society
1 W. Market Street, Lewistown, PA 17044
Office: 717 - 242 - 1022

At left, top: Nolte Studio on Market Square, c. 1900; old Mifflin County Airport, 1947 air show; T. F. Gibboney family photo, believed to be taken below the woolen mill, c. 1910 (see p. 16).

Annual *Picture the Past* Calendar Project for Elementary Students

Mifflin County 4th graders have received society calendars since 2001, at no cost to the students or parents.

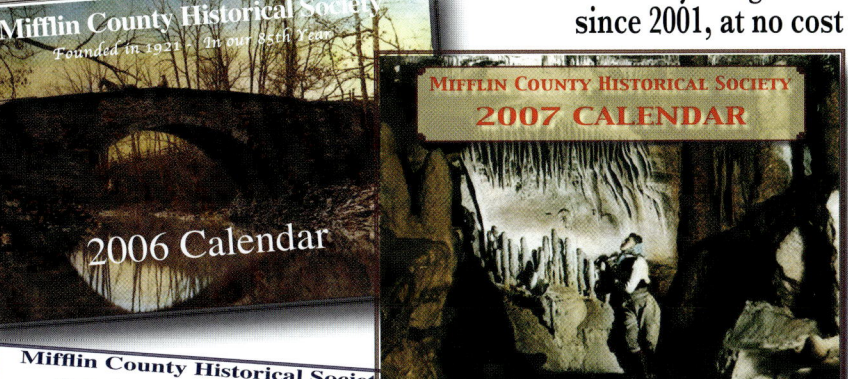

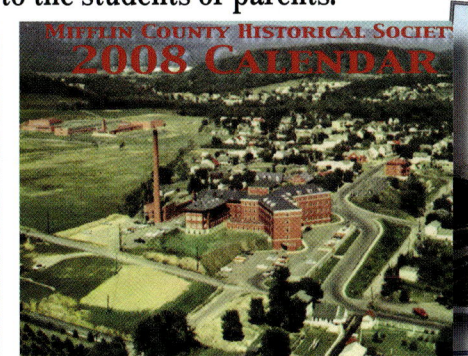

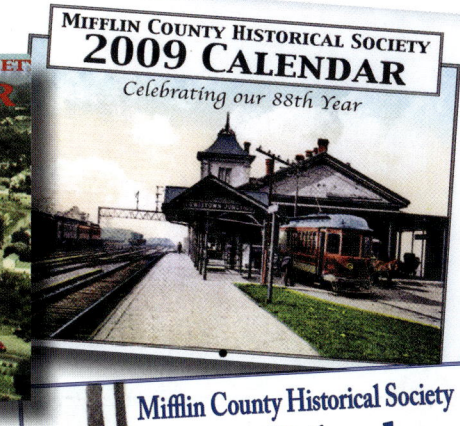

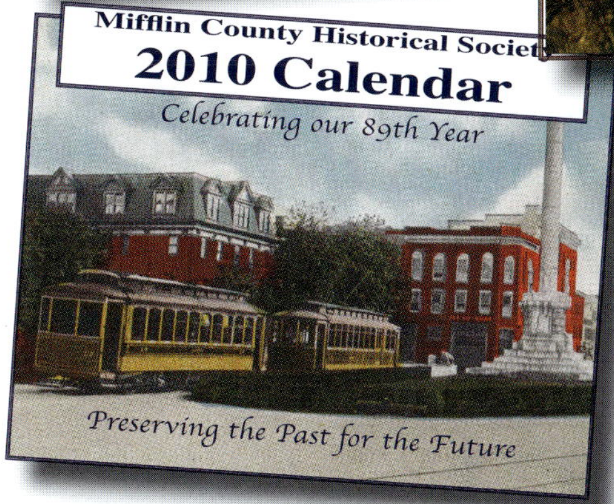

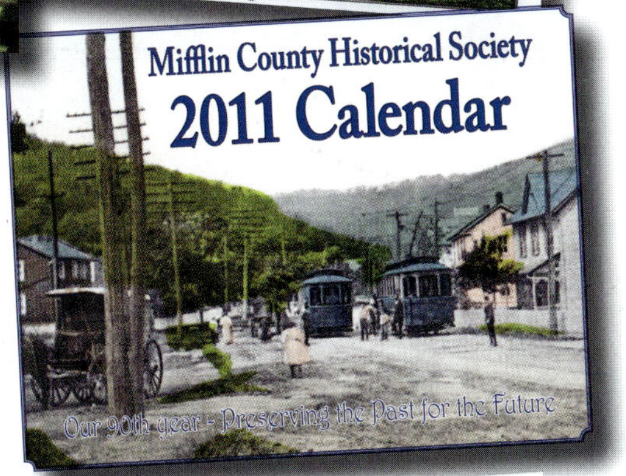

One way the Mifflin County Historical Society has actively spread the story of our unique history is through the annual calendar project. Individual and business patrons give financial support during the annual calendar drive. This underwrites printing costs, and allows for free distribution to students in Mifflin County's public and private schools. Over 5,500 students and their families have glimpsed the county's heritage through dozens of the society's vintage archive photos. Many individuals have also shared treasured family images that have appeared in the "Picture the Past" calendars since 2001.

Contact the historical society if you would like to help.

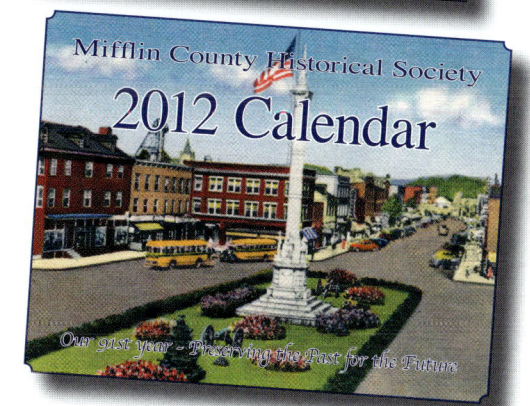

The 2014 cover was taken from the attic at McCoy House, 17 N. Main Street, Lewistown. Photographer Nathaniel Thierwechter snapped the shot New Year's Eve, 2012.

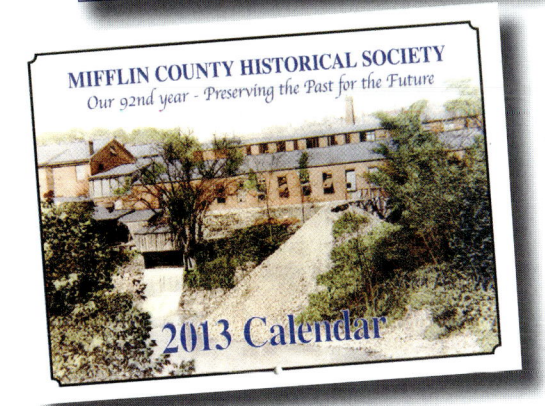

All calendar sales benefit the Mifflin County Historical Society.

Contact the historical society if you would like to support the project.